List of Tables, Boxes, Graphs and Figures

Preface

There is strong evidence that older people want to remain living in their own homes and communities as independently as possible for as long as possible. This preference has been accepted by successive Governments as a key policy objective. Yet this objective is nowhere near achievement. This is reflected in our under-developed community care system, which is crisis driven, lacks sufficient co-ordination and resources and does not afford older people the choice, independence and autonomy they seek and deserve.

The present report, which was prepared by an NESF Project Team, focuses on examining the current set of choices available to older people in respect of health and social care and identifies gaps in the continuum of care that currently exist.

There is broad acceptance that care is a central social concern. The NESF has recently published its report on *Early Childhood Care and Education* (NESF Report Number 31), which focused on the development and implementation of a policy framework for children from birth to age six. This current report looks at care in old age and is designed to complement other issues being addressed under the National Agreement, *Sustaining Progress,* such as the work of the Working Group on policy options for the financing of long-term care for older people and the pilot Home Care Grant Scheme; and the care issues raised by the Oireachtas Committee on Social and Family Affairs.

For this purpose, the report develops a vision of what is needed to be done so as to make living at home in older age a reality for all, and one that moves towards person-centred community care responses. It also identifies the priority actions that are necessary to achieve this vision. This proposed shift in policy approach is necessary because:

- **OUR SOCIETY IS CHANGING,** in make-up as the number of older people increase, but also our families and familial relationships and traditional support structures are altering; and

- **OUR EXPECTATIONS ARE CHANGING,** service users are becoming more empowered and services are expected to be more consumer-driven and quality-based in the future.

In line with its mandate from Government, this report was discussed at an NESF Plenary Session in late September in the Royal Hospital Kilmainham. This was attended by Members and a wide variety of guests representing concerned individuals and groups with practical experience on the ground, Government Departments, State Agencies and those who made submissions to help us in our work. The Team's approach was well received at the Plenary and the many valuable contributions helped to subsequently strengthen and clarify the Team's final recommendations.

The NESF would like to record its appreciation to all those who contributed to this report, particularly those who made written submission or met with the Project Team. The members of the Project Team are also to be thanked for their hard work and commitment, and the Project Team Leader, Professor Eamon O'Shea, NUI, Galway for his sterling work in facilitating the many contributions made and for bringing the work to a successful conclusion as well as the NESF Secretariat.

October 2005

Executive Summary

This Executive Summary is presented in three interconnecting parts.

The first part outlines the context in which the Project Team on Care for Older People undertook its work. The second gives a brief overview of the report, and the third part details the Team's priority recommendations, which are summarised below.

Summary of Key Recommendations

- Bring public spending on care services for older people up to at least the OECD average of 1 per cent of GDP over the next five years, at an additional cost of €500 million

- Develop a National Action Plan on Ageing

- Root out ageism and promote positive ageing

- Clarify entitlement to core community care services and introduce unified and holistic assessment of need

- Increase financial support for homecare

- Strengthen co-ordination, implement care and case management

- Develop standards of care across the system and emphasise quality of life outcomes

- Positive ageing training should be delivered to all relevant staff (policy-makers, managers and care staff)

- Maintain and develop housing stock

- Develop a National Strategy on Caring

The Project complements work already underway by the Working Group established under the National Agreement, *Sustaining Progress*, to identify the policy options for a financially sustainable system of long-term care, which is due to report shortly.

1.   Care in the community is not the reality it should be

Care is a central policy concern. The NESF has recently published its report on *Early Childhood Care and Education* (NESF Report Number 31) and in this report the focus is on care for older people. In setting out a vision of care services for older people, the Team was informed by the strong preference of older people that they should be able to remain living in their own homes as independently as possible for as long as possible. This has been official Government policy since the publication of *The Years Ahead: A Policy for the Elderly* in 1988, but the evidence suggests that much more needs to be done to make this a reality. In this regard, the work of the National Council on Ageing and Older People has been instrumental in identifying barriers to affecting real change in the lives of older people.

A key barrier to achieving official policy has been the weakness in policy implementation. The Team's views on this barrier are multi-faceted:

Implementation barriers

- Relatively low social spending on services for older people
- Funding not consistent with policy objectives
- Equality issues not adequately addressed
- Lack of clarity on entitlement
- Strategy needs to be up-dated

• **BELOW AVERAGE SPENDING ON SERVICES FOR OLDER PEOPLE.** Our levels of social spending on social protection are low by EU and OECD standards considering our levels of wealth, and this is particularly so for services relating to old age. Estimated public expenditure here on care services for older people in 2004 was just under one billion euro, which equates to 0.67 per cent of GDP. OECD estimates for 2000 suggests that public expenditure on care services for older people in OECD countries averaged at just under 1 per cent of GDP (OECD, 2005, Table 1.2). Bringing Ireland up to the OECD average would entail an additional expenditure of €500 million on care services for older people. Even allowing for age structure differences between Ireland and the rest of the OECD countries, an additional expenditure of this magnitude will be necessary in the medium-term to meet the Government's own targets of increased investment in community care and improved quality of care and quality of life for older people in long-stay care. The economic framework is one where our economy is performing well, and forecast to continue to grow at 5 per cent per year for the next five years to the end of the current decade, with close to full employment levels (Economic and Social Research Institute, 2005). This robust economic outlook provides the opportunity and the resources for investment in developing community-based care responses as recommended in this report.

- **PERVERSE INVESTMENT INCENTIVES.** It is also clear that the funding of services for older people has not always been wholly consistent with the policy objective of encouraging community-based responses. Considerable resources have been invested in nursing home care responses, some of which was unnecessary, not wanted and inappropriate. For many older people, inappropriate or unnecessary admission to acute or long-stay residential care could have been avoided or delayed by greater development of community services and use of preventative and proactive approaches.

- **EQUALITY FOR OLDER PEOPLE.** In its earlier report on *Implementing Equality for Older People: Implementation Issues* (Report Number 29), which built on the Equality Authority's report on these issues (Equality Authority, 2002), the NESF outlined how an equality agenda for older people might best be implemented. This current report builds on the framework outlined there and the work of the National Council on Ageing and Older People and other groups representing the interests of older people. Progress on achieving a more age-friendly society and care system cannot be achieved unless ageism in all its forms is rooted out of our system and equitable services to meet older people's needs are developed.

- **SERVICE ENTITLEMENT.** The majority of older people remain active and independent; however, it is increasingly clear that services also play an important role in helping others to remain independent for longer. Our services have developed in a patchy fashion; they lack unity in terms of coverage and access, grounding in needs-assessment and systematic data gathering and analysis. This was a strong issue to emerge from the written submissions received by the Team. The commitment in the Health Strategy *Quality and Fairness: A Health System for You* that eligibility arrangements will be simplified and clarified and the establishment of the Health Service Executive provide a unique opportunity to move services forward to achieve a more even response to need, but one which still allows for local-level flexibility.

- **STRATEGIC STATEMENT ON AGEING.** The modern approach to public policy development places considerable emphasis on the development of strategies to inform funding priorities and actions. In relation to older people, the current strategy is almost twenty years old and requires up-dating, particularly to move away from a central focus on the medical model of ageing, which addresses ageing in terms of increasing infirmity, to one which places more emphasis on the social aspects of ageing, which enables older people to continue to contribute to and participate in society. It would be important that any such strategy would be developed with a clear understanding of what older people themselves want and what they need. This current report provides a starting point to develop strategy.

2. Overview of the Report

The Team's Report is divided into 8 Sections. A brief overview of each Section is now provided and then the Team's recommendations are outlined.

Contents

1   Background and policy setting

2   Rooting out ageism

3   Making living at home possible

4   Legal aspects of community care

5   Co-ordinated approaches

6   The most vulnerable

7   Enhancing quality of care and quality of life

8   Delivering change

Section 1 details the purpose and working methods of the Team and the domestic and international policy developments in the context of ageing populations. It draws attention to the slow pace of implementation of domestic policy for older people and the shift internationally to more person-centred, home-based responses and more universal public provision, with a greater emphasis on making services more consumer-directed and standards-driven. The nature of informal care is also changing. The Section then examines three over-arching issues. The first relates to the different dimensions of quality: quality of life, quality of care and quality of outcome; the second focuses on valuing older people's participation in society, to counteract negative stereotyping of ageing as increased dependency, but stressing instead the need for healthy ageing, greater social inclusion and representation of older people, comprehensive services and making our living environment more age-friendly. In the third and final over-arching theme, the Team concentrates on the barriers to better community care responses, which are addressed throughout the report.

Section 2 gives priority to rooting out ageism in our society, as it inhibits older people's full and dignified social participation. The Team provides evidence of both positive and negative discrimination, arguing that positive discrimination can be supported if it counteracts negative discrimination or promotes equality of opportunity or caters for a person's special needs. The research evidence leads to the conclusion that ageism and negative discrimination are serious blockages to progress and the Team recommends an action plan to tackle it.

In **Section 3,** the Team addresses a core aspect of its work: making living at home possible. In this Section, extending older people's choices, supporting their independence and empowerment, developing flexible responses to need and supporting carers are discussed in turn. The Section focuses on how services should become more person-centred, and move away from the current 'one-size-fits-all' approach. Two specific areas are outlined in more detail, that of housing and transport. In looking at the issue of community-based provision more generally, it draws from UK research which found that low-level supports, if provided at the right time, can have better outcomes for older people, compared to interventions which only kick-start at crisis points. The Team calls for a rebalancing of care supports to support home living and strongly supports the concept of community-based subventions in this context, particularly for those on the margins between community and residential care. It also supports the view that carers are a core element of any community care strategy and that a national strategy for caring is now required.

Section 4 deals with two related issues around the lack of a legal base to community care services for older people, which have been identified as an implementation barrier. First the potential positives and drawbacks of a rights-based approach are examined and then the practical barriers to community groups developing locally-based community care responses for older people are discussed. This approach was taken to mean that there should be legal clarity about services, that services should be consistent and fair and provided in a timely manner.

On the one hand it is argued, for example, that it is up to governments to decide on resource allocation and that rights-based legislation would be likely to lead to resources being wasted in litigation. On the other hand, the absence of clear rights to services diminishes active citizenship. The different aspects of rights are explored, for example, the right to a remedy, to information, to an assessment of need and that this approach does not mean that the services must be provided free of charge. Barriers to community groups developing local responses are then explored by the Team, and poor co-ordination between health and housing authorities and overly narrow funding sources are identified as the main barriers, rather than legal issues. The new health legislation underlines the importance of more integrated services.

Section 5 develops further the theme of integration and focuses on the issue of co-ordinated approaches to the planning and delivery of services. This has positive returns in terms of efficiency and effectiveness. As part of public service modernisation, greater emphasis is now placed on more integrated approaches to service delivery and the development of cross-Departmental problem-solving approaches. The inter-Departmental Group on the Needs of Older People, for example, is identified by the Team as an important initiative, but one which needs to be strengthened to become more effective. Planning structures at a local level also need to be inclusive of older people.

The concepts of care and case management, a more integrated approach to care planning and delivery, are then examined. Staff training is identified as a key to its successful implementation. A unified assessment of need to collect information on a person's situation, which would also take account of their ability to pay for services, is also supported. Finally, in this Section, the Team looks at how community and residential care can be better integrated. This involves a remodelling of the role of institutional care to favour respite, rehabilitation and re-integration; the development of more intermediate care between primary and specialist services; and the better linking of community-based services to hospital and institutional settings, for example around the point of discharge from hospital.

The NESF has a particular mandate to consider the needs of those most vulnerable or marginalised and **Section 6** considers the position of particular groups whose vulnerability may have arisen early in life, or may be age-related or caused by a combination of both life events and the ageing process. While there is consider-able diversity in old age, there are also some common features. Many older people are healthy and socially active. While they may be cash poor, they are also less likely than other groups to report that they have to go without basic items because they cannot afford them. The Team then highlights the following vulner-able groups, while recognising that these are neither exhaustive nor mutually exclusive: the homeless; those from the Traveller Community; ethnic minorities; older people with disabilities; those experiencing elder abuse; 'eccentrics' in the community; those who are lesbian, gay or bi-sexual; those experiencing social isolation, particularly in rural areas; those leaving institutional care; the very old; and those who have suffered bereavement. Particular attention is given to the vulnerability of those with dementia and the need to implement a person-centred model to caring for them.

The issue of quality is central to **Section 7** and it begins by outlining current developments in relation to accreditation and the promotion of quality care in residential settings. Emphasis is given to the need for consistency across different care settings and services, to base standards on consultation and to view standards as the route to continuous improvement. The importance of quality care environments is stressed, but even more important is the need for high quality staff to deliver services. The Team then considers what makes for a good old age. Drawing from UK research, the importance of interdependence, of being able to give and to receive is given particular emphasis. In residential settings, the importance of independence, choice and autonomy are flagged, while accepting that this involves a certain amount of risk taking. The value of health promotion is also underlined in this Section and its on-going development encouraged.

Section 8 focuses on what needs to be done to deliver change and to achieve implementation, particularly for those who are most vulnerable. The Team begins by outlining why change to the status quo is needed and what this will entail:

- emphasising older people's independence and ensuring choice and access to a core of high-quality services when needed;

- consulting with older people regarding their needs and responding in a timely and appropriate fashion;

- collecting the necessary information to inform service planning, at an individual to national level; and

- valuing innovation and best practice.

Written Submissions

The Team called for written submissions and received over 140 replies.
Here are some extracts:

- We would like to see a greater consensus emerging in public life about the fact that ageism and age discrimination exist and greater will is needed to tackle it.

- There is a required shift in mindset in terms of looking at the person and their contribution to society rather than they being perceived as a cost factor to the State.

- Government should adopt a strategy framework for housing and care for the elderly.

- A single assessment process in relation to care management could minimise duplication by the various professionals and service providers.

The Team prioritises the next steps to achieve this change and reviews the financial implications and information requirements for progress. Given the complexity and diversity of our current systems of care, and the resistance and power of inertia, the changes recommended by the Team to modernise care for older people will require considerable leadership to move forward. But this is vital if we are to respond more effectively to the emerging social and economic context outlined in this report. Changing our approach to care for older people will have very significant benefits for older people themselves, by enhancing their quality of life, but it will also benefit society more generally by increasing and sustaining older people's ability to participate and contribute to society, through family, community or workplace settings. Key actors are identified to drive the necessary institutional and structural changes required and mechanisms are recommended to monitor progress and measure outcomes.

The Team's priority recommendations are now outlined.

3. Delivering Change: Prioritised Recommendations

The Team's recommendations are collated below for easy reference. Where possible, the lead implementation agents are identified and timeframes indicated. The recommendations relate to actions required in the short to medium-term. Many of them should be well underway if not completed within a 12 month timeframe. A key factor in driving implementation will be leadership to simultan-eously deliver the mindset change and additional resources to achieve a new approach to care services for older people, underpinned by the principles of independence, autonomy and choice (numbers refer to corresponding paragraph numbers in the report).

1.14 INCREASE PUBLIC SPENDING ON CARE FOR OLDER PEOPLE TO AT LEAST OECD AVERAGE

The Team recommends that public spending on care services for older people should be increased over the next five years to at least the OECD average of 1 per cent of GDP. Reaching this target would entail an additional minimum expenditure of €500 million per year on services for older people in this country. This additional funding should be ring-fenced for these services and there should be an in-built emphasis on measuring outcomes.

1.28 DEVELOP A NATIONAL STRATEGY ON AGEING

The Team recommends that a New National Strategy on Ageing should be developed by the Inter-Departmental Group on the Needs of Older People, to be chaired by the Department of the Taoiseach to provide the strategic underpinnings for change. The Strategy should cover all service areas of relevance to older people and include consideration of the following:

- the status of older people and their contribution to society;

- baseline data and information for planning;

- current resource allocation;

- an audit of current service provision;

- cross-cutting issues such as co-ordination, needs assessment, standards; and

- implementation, for example, the value in establishing a National Office for Ageing (based on international experience and the lessons from the establishment of the National Children's Office).

Moving ahead on the Team's other recommendations does not need to be delayed until the completion of this Strategy; rather its focus should be on implementation. This Strategy should be completed by end 2006.

2.12 – 2.16 Root out Ageism and Promote Positive Ageing

The Team recommends that a National Strategy to Root out Ageism and Promote Positive Ageing should be developed at three inter-connecting levels.

At **Government level,** a Statement that ageism and age discrimination should be eliminated should be published. The promotion of an age-friendly society should be mainstreamed in national strategies (e.g the National Development Programme). These are immediate priorities.

At the **Policy level** a Working Group on Positive Ageing should be established by the Department of Health and Children on publication of the Team's report. It should have a broad membership of Government Departments, Social Partners and experts to:

- audit existing Departmental policy and procedures and develop a strategic response;

- consult with older people and others;

- promote positive ageing in both the public and private sectors;

- develop national anti-ageism guidelines and advise on age-proofing; and

- monitor progress and produce an annual report.

This should be linked to the **Delivery level,** where relevant statutory service providers, for example, the Health Service Executive and Local Authorities, should pay greater attention to the needs of older people through:

- better inter-agency liaison at a senior level on positive ageing issues;

- the inclusion of age equality as a cross-cutting theme in strategic planning;

- age-proofing and auditing services from an age impact perspective and using administrative data to check for age discrimination;

- raising public awareness of ageism issues;

- including older people in customer groups;

- staff training; and

- supporting local initiatives.

In addition, the County and City Development Boards should develop positive ageing approaches. Progress should be reported to the National Working Group on Positive Ageing.

3.7 – 3.11 A MORE STRATEGIC ROLE FOR HOUSING

The Team recommends that the Department of the Environment, Heritage and Local Government should develop and strengthen its on-going evaluation and assessment of the housing schemes, focusing in particular on efficiency and equity issues and older people's quality of life outcomes.

The Team recommends that the Department of the Environment, Heritage and Local Government should undertake research to assess older people's housing preferences and identify and address potential barriers or disincentives to their moving to the accommodation which best fits their needs.

The Team recommends that the role of assisted and supported housing should be expanded as a housing option for older people, particularly where it supports independent living and a continuum of care. This will require the development of a strategic framework for housing and care, which should address funding issues (capital and current), services and supports, planning issues and co-ordination between health and housing sectors.

3.25 SUPPORT FOR HOMECARE

The Team recommends that community-based financial or other supports for services should be made more widespread, focusing initially on high-dependent older people in the community and drawing on best practice from the pilot programme of care for older people (under the National Agreement *Sustaining Progress*); and that consideration should be given on equity and efficiency grounds to re-balancing the financial supports to different people in different situations (e.g. community and residential settings).

3.30 A NATIONAL STRATEGY FOR CARERS

The Team recommends that the Departments of Health and Children and Social and Family Affairs should jointly establish a broad-based group (including relevant Social Partners, Carers groups and experts) to develop a National Strategy for Carers. This should give particular attention to the specific needs of older carers and should be completed within 12 months.

4.41 CLARIFY ENTITLEMENTS TO COMMUNITY CARE AND HOLISTIC ASSESSMENT OF NEED

The Team recommends that the Department of Health and Children should clarify older people's entitlement to community care services, for example, core services such as the home help service, meals-on-wheels, day care, respite care, therapeutic/paramedic services and assisted and supported housing within the next six months. The Department should also commit to the expansion of these core services to become more comprehensive. In keeping with the recently enacted Disability Act, 2005, the Team also recommends that older people should have a right to a holistic assessment of their needs.

5.11 Strengthen cross-Departmental Co-ordination and Planning

The Team recommends that the Inter-Departmental Group on the Needs of Older People should be widened and strengthened to take on a stronger cross-Departmental remit with representatives at Assistant Secretary level and supported by a permanent and senior level Secretariat. This Group should:

- develop a National Strategy on Ageing;

- consider the structures, legislation and funding requirements and allocation needed to underpin cross-Departmental co-ordination and integrated planning; and

- support innovative approaches to local-level service co-ordination and disseminate good practice.

5.13 Make issues affecting older people more central to local planning and delivery

The Team recommends that:

- Older people should have an active role in planning and service delivery at local level on an on-going basis, through consultation and participation.

- Issues of specific concern to older people should be addressed by local and regional planning fora, for example, the HSE Advisory Panels, the Strategic Planning Committees, Vocational Education Committees and the County and City Development Boards and older people should be specifically represented on these fora.

- Greater emphasis should be given to the role of co-ordinating staff in service planning and delivery and all service delivery staff should receive training on integrated service responses, standards should be set and best practice disseminated.

- Data gathering systems should be developed which are person-centred and have the capacity to be collated and analysed to plan appropriate responses for groups of older people (e.g. at community level or additional needs level).

- IT solutions should be developed to promote co-ordination and integration and also to promote assistive technology for independent living.

- The development of innovative approaches to service co-ordination (such as joint planning and budget sharing) should be supported and lessons learnt, disseminated and mainstreamed.

5.18 – 5.19 EMBED CARE AND CASE MANAGEMENT PRINCIPLES IN THE CARE SYSTEM

The Team recommends that the Department of Health and Children and the HSE should ensure that care and case management principles, philosophies and approaches are embedded across the community care system and at the point of admission to and discharge from residential and acute care services. The Team also recommends that a unified and holistic assessment process of establishing people's needs for services should be introduced as a priority.

7.14 INSPECT AND ENHANCE ALL STANDARDS OF CARE

The Team recommends that:

- the remit of the Social Services Inspectorate should be extended on a statutory basis to include all care settings for older people (residential, community and home-based; private, State or community/voluntary provision), with the necessary staff and financial resources;

- Inspectors should be adequately trained and inspection findings should be published;

- there should be sanctions for non-compliance with standards;

- the principles of autonomy, empowerment and person-centredness should inform the development and implementation of the standards;

- standards should be clear, adequate and agreed, and developed in consultation with users;

- the Department of Health and Children should develop policy in relation to standards of care for older people in acute hospital settings;

- proactive development of higher standards is required to further move care towards quality of life measures; and

- standards should be developed and applied across all service levels – from front-line service delivery, organisation of care, planning / integration and strategic development.

I

Introduction and Policy Context

Purpose of the Report

1.1 ● The focus of this report is on community care for older people. 'Older' here refers to those sixty-five years of age or over. In adopting this traditional age cut-off point, however, the Project Team was conscious that chronological age is not an accurate determinant of people's needs or preferences as there are dramatic differences in the health status, participation and levels of independence among older people of the same age. A key point that the Team will be making in this report is that an over-reliance on age cut-off points in framing policy and practice is an ineffective way to respond to needs, and one that can be discriminatory and counterproductive to positive ageing.

1.2 ● A second and related point the Team wishes to emphasise from the outset is that many older people are very independent and active and may not require or want any formal 'community care' services in its broadest definition (see below). In keeping with the mandate given to the NESF by Government, the Team has focused particularly on those most marginal-ised and at risk of social exclusion. For this group, community care services undoubtedly play a central role in framing people's choices and supporting their preferences and have the potential to positively impact on their quality of life.

1.3 ● This Section of the report introduces the work of the Project Team and then examines four contextual areas:

- the policy context;

- dimensions of quality: quality of life, quality of care and quality of outcome;

- valuing older peoples participation in society; and

- barriers to achieving better community care.

Project Team's Methods of Work

1.4 ● The Team was representative of a broad range of interests and organisations. Membership of the Team was as follows:

Project Team Leader	**Dr Eamon O'Shea,** National University of Ireland, Galway
Strand 1	Senator **Geraldine Feeney, Fianna Fáil** Senator **Kate Walsh,** Progressive Democrats Deputy **Jerry Cowley,** Independent
Strand 2	**Ian Martin,** Irish Business and Employers Confederation **Michael O'Halloran,** Irish Congress of Trade Unions **Mary McGreal,** Irish Farmers' Association
Strand 3	**Sheila Cronin,** Conference of Religious of Ireland **Maria Fox,** Disability Federation of Ireland **Robin Webster,** Age Action Ireland
Strand 4	**David Wolfe,** Department of Health and Children* **Bob Carroll,** National Council on Ageing and Older People **Ger Barron,** General Council of County Councils **Mo Flynn,** Health Service Executive **Cáit Keane,** Independent
Secretariat	**David Silke**

*The Team would like to acknowledge the contribution of Mr David Wolfe, who died during the course of this project.

1.5 ● The Team adopted a positive holistic view of ageing and later life, which stressed the importance of older people's full participation in economic, social and cultural life (see Annex 2). It developed a vision of what is to be achieved to make living at home in old age a clearer reality for older people, based on a bias towards person-centred community care responses.

1.6 ● In keeping with this vision, throughout its work the Team emphasised:

• the positive contribution of older people and the need for their greater participation in defining policy;

• promoting positive ageing, independence and equity for older people in economic, social and cultural life, particularly the most vulnerable;

• separating 'dependency' from 'situations of dependency' for older people;

• examining current resource allocation for older people in community and long-stay settings;

- promoting the social integration of dependent older people through the development of integrated primary and community care models, life-adaptable accommodation, public transport, lifelong learning, technology, etc;

- the legal dimensions, both in terms of a 'rights-based' approach and legislative barriers to greater community participation in care;

- the importance of solidarity at family, neighbour, community, voluntary and statutory level;

- exploring the meaning of quality of life for vulnerable older people in community and long-stay care settings, including people with dementia;

- examining the nature and process of policy formulation and policy implementation for older people; and

- the impact of age discrimination and how it should be tackled.

1.7 ● As part of its working methods the Team:

- met on fourteen occasions;

- called for written submissions from interested parties and received over 140 replies (see Annex 3);

- commissioned a Policy Paper on the Legal Aspects of Community Care;

- met with a wide range of individuals and organisations; and

- visited a number of care sites and spoke with residents and staff.

1.8 ● A central question throughout this report is: *what changes are required in policy and practice to ensure that older people can live as independently as possible in their own homes and communities for longer, if that is their wish?* The focus of the Team's work was on the current set of choices available to older people in respect of health and social care in Ireland and to identify any gaps in the continuum of care that currently exist. As a result, a second feature of this work has been to focus on policy implementation — the degree to which current policy is being implemented and what barriers exist to achieving policy objectives.

1.9 ● A third and overarching aspect of the Team's work has been to consider the impact of policies from an equality perspective. This follows on from the earlier work of the Equality Authority on *Implementing Equality for Older People (2002)* which contained a comprehensive strategy for change, built around the following key strategies or actions:

- age-proofing or assessing decisions made for their impact on older people;

- positive action to address a past history of exclusion of older people;

- participation by older people and their organisations in decisions that affect them;

• training in age awareness and skills in combating ageism; and

• underpinning access to key services through legislative entitlement (Equality Authority, 2002).

The NESF established a Project Team to identify potential implementation barriers and challenges to fulfilling the main priority recommendations in the Equality Authority report and to comment and make recommendations on how these could be addressed, which was published in 2003 — *Equality Policies for Older People: Implementation Issues* (Report Number 30, July 2003). The NESF called for a systematic implementation of the Equality Authority's recommendations and:

• the introduction of on-going mechanisms to monitor progress;

• greater investment to tackle ageism and social attitudes;

• better co-ordination of cross-cutting issues;

• 'older people within their community' should be a core value tested before any alternative policy responses are considered or adopted;

• research and administrative data should be age-proofed and upper age limits removed; and

• Departments should age-proof policies and programmes.

The NESF will return to assess progress in relation to the implementation of the recommendations in this report in its Fifth Periodic Report.

1.10 ● A final aspect of the Team's work is the economic framework and particularly the current levels of investment in care for older people. The United Nations recently ranked Ireland 8th in the world in relation to human development for 2003, up from 10th position in 2002 and from 17th position in 2000. This ranking is based on three dimensions, namely: life expectancy, adult literacy rates and GDP per capita. Ireland ranked second in the world, after Luxembourg, in terms of GDP or the wealth we produce per capita (United Nations Development Programme, 2005).[1]

1.11 ● International comparisons of social spending are difficult. The data which is available indicates that in absolute terms we are low spenders on social protection (which covers cash transfers and services) compared to the EU 15 average, and particularly so in relation to our level of wealth. For example, our social spending per capita in 2001 was only 60.5 per cent of the EU 15 average, adjusting for differences in the cost of living (i.e. in a common purchasing power standard, PPS). Only Spain and Portugal spend proportionally less (Eurostat, 2004). If this figure is further broken down to examine spending on old age, as is shown in Table 1.1, we rank lowest of our EU 15 neighbours in terms of our social spending per person (National Economic and Social Council, 2005, p109).

---

[1] *It is argued that using Gross Domestic Product (GDP) exaggerates Ireland's true wealth and that Gross National Product (GNP) is a more accurate measure to use. The gap between the two measures is significant - about 20 per cent - because GDP includes the value of the economic activity undertaken by multinational companies. To adopt a GNP measure, however, would overlook the significance of the tax revenue which multinationals contribute and, on a more practical level, restrict comparisons with other countries where GDP is the accepted norm (see NESF, 2004, p.132; NESC, 2005, p.137).*

Table 1.1 Social Expenditure per Person in PPS
on Old Age (aged 65+)

Country	Social Expenditure on Old Age per person aged 65+ in PPS, 2001
Denmark	19,516
Austria	18,648
Netherlands	18,592
Germany	17,837
Italy	17,199
France	16,916
United Kingdom	16,495
Sweden	14,840
Belgium	13,048
Finland	12,050
Greece	10,782
Portugal	10,167
Spain	9,771
Ireland	6,439

Source : various sources cited in National Economic and Social Council, 2005, p.109, Table 4.7
Note: PPS refers to common purchasing power standard.

1.12 ● Table 1.2 overleaf shows that estimated public expenditure on care services for older people in both community and residential settings in 2004 was just under one billion euro, more than half of which was spent on residential care in public and private long-stay settings (caring for about 5 per cent of older people). This level of overall spending equates to 0.67% of GDP. OECD estimates for 2000 suggest that public expenditure on care services in OECD countries on home care and in institutions (excluding acute services in hospitals) averaged at just under 1 per cent of GDP (OECD, 2005, Table 1.2). Bringing Ireland up to the OECD average would entail an additional expenditure of €500 million on services for older people here. Even allowing for age structure differences between Ireland and the rest of the OECD countries, an additional expenditure of this magnitude will be necessary in the medium-term to meet the Government's own targets of increased investment in community care and improved quality of care and quality of life for older people in long-stay care.

Table 1.2 Care Services for Older People:
Current Spending on Programmes and Services,
2004–2005

	Provisional outturn 2004 €000	Estimated Expenditure 2005 €000
Long Stay Residential Hospitals	409,923	428,826
Community Residences and Day Care Centre	339,938	353,335
Nursing Home Subvention	113,984	140,040
Home Help Service	103,978	112,236
Other Services for Older People	31,994	34,196
Total	999,817	1,068,633

Source : Communication from the Department of Health and Children.

1.13 ● The Team acknowledges that achieving the care vision outlined in this report has cost implications. The economic framework is one where our economy is performing well, with forecasts from the Economic and Social Research Institute predicting continued grow at 5 per cent per year for the next five years to the end of the current decade, with close to full employment levels (McCoy, *et al,* 2005; Bergin, *et al,* 2003). This robust economic outlook provides the opportunity and the resources for the investment in developing community-based care responses as recommended in this report.

1.14 ● The Team recommends that public spending on care services for older people should be increased over the next five years to at least the OECD average of 1 per cent of GDP. Reaching this target would entail an additional minimum expenditure of The Team recommends €500 million per year on services for older people in this country. This additional funding should be ring-fenced for these services and there should be an in-built emphasis on measuring outcomes.

Policy Context

1.15 ● *The Care of the Aged Report (1968)* marked a shift away from institutional care (County Homes) as the default response to addressing older people's care needs to one based more on enabling older people who can do so to live in their own homes. *Twenty years later, The Years Ahead: a Policy for the Elderly (1988)* reiterated the underlying philosophy of this earlier report. *The Years Ahead* remains the most significant national policy document exclusively dedicated to older people. It recommended that the objectives of public policy in regard to older people should be:

• to maintain them in dignity and independence in their own home;

• to restore those older people who become ill or dependent to independence at home;

• to encourage and support the care of older people in their own community by family, neighbours and voluntary bodies in every way possible; and

• to provide a high quality of hospital and residential care for older people when they can no longer be maintained in dignity and independence at home.

The report listed seven objectives for services for older people, which are discussed in more detail below (Para 1.54).

1.16 ● *The Years Ahead* is now almost twenty years old. This is testament to its significant influence on policy development in this area, but this in turn also raises questions about the degree to which policy objectives have been achieved and whether *The Years Ahead* framework is still valid today. A comprehensive evaluation of the implementation of the report was undertaken for the National Council on Ageing and Older People (NCAOP) ten years after its publication. It concluded, in 1998, that *The Years Ahead* remained a significant influence on the care of older people in this country, but that, by then, it was no longer an adequate blue print for the development of older people's health and social services. The NCAOP observed that:

• *The Years Ahead* did not adopt a person-centred approach, as we understand it today, with an emphasis on tailored packages of care to meet the particular needs of the individual, but rather on norms of service provision to meet the projected needs of the older population.

• Interdepartmental co-ordination (between the Departments of Health, of Social Welfare and of the Environment particularly) and coordination at the local level (between health boards and local authorities) as was recommended has not yet happened in any systematic way; this has impeded the achievement of policy objectives.

1.17 ● The NCAOP's evaluation also identified obstacles to the implementation of *The Years Ahead* recommendations, which are worth listing here as potential barriers which future proposals may also have to overcome:

• *The Years Ahead* had no statutory basis, and the recommendations it made for legal underpinning of core services such as home helps and meals on wheels and co-ordination services were not implemented;

• in the years immediately following the publication of the report, sufficient funding was not made available to develop services as envisaged and the transfer of resources to community care in line with the principles espoused in it had not occurred. Indeed increased funding

in the early 1990s was channelled towards services for children, on foot of
the enactment of the Child Care Act in 1991 and on subvention of nursing
home care, on foot of the Nursing Home Act, 1990;

- the core services required to achieve the objectives set out in *The Years
  Ahead* were not provided in a consistent and equitable basis across the
  country; and

- there was a lack of information about the report and its recommendations, particularly among those outside the health services, such as local
  authorities (Ruddle, *et al,* 1998).

1.18 ● The Health Strategy, *Quality and Fairness: A Health System for You
(2001),* outlined an Action Plan for the development of health services,
including the development of services for older people. It set out four
goals, each with specific actions relating to older people, as detailed in Box
1.1 overleaf. It will be noted that the Strategy involved a number of specific
actions relating to strategy planning to respond to the needs of older
people, the expansion of services, clarification of eligibility arrangements,
funding for community groups, feedback mechanisms for older people and
their carers, greater integration of care services and supports to older
people and more emphasis on quality and standards.

Box 1.1

Health Strategy: Actions for Older People

Action 1   **Better health for everyone**

- Development of a co-ordinated action plan
- Funding for community groups
- Implementation of the Health Promotion Strategy for Older People
- Implementation of action plan on dementia

Action 2   **Fair access**

- Eligibility arrangements will be simplified and clarified
- Introduction of integrated care subvention scheme to maximise support for homecare
- Introduction of grant for respite care (two weeks per annum)
- Financing of long-term care proposals to be brought forward

Action 3   **Responsiveness and appropriate care delivery**

- Integrated approach to care planning for individuals
- Regional advisory panels to include older customers and carers
- Support for community and voluntary activity to support informal care giving and foster volunteerism
- Increased capacity in community, hospital and residential care

Action 4   **High performance**

- Remit of Social Services Inspectorate to include residential care
- National care standards will be prepared

Source : Department of Health and Children (2001) Quality and Fairness: A Health System for You. p.150-151.

1.19 ● Actions taken to date towards implementation of the *Health Strategy* include:

- additional revenue funding was allocated to Services for Older People for the development of services — €130m from 2002 to 2005;
- old age psychiatry services have been expanded;
- dedicated dementia units for older people are being established by the Health Service Executive;
- a Working Group was established by the Department of Health and Children to review the operation and administration of the Nursing Home Subvention Scheme on foot of a review of the Scheme commissioned by the Departments of Health and Children and Finance and carried out by Dr Eamon O'Shea, National University of Ireland, Galway;

- pilot home subvention schemes have been established in a number of Health Service Executive areas throughout the country and the National Nursing Home Team has been requested by the Department of Health and Children to develop a national scheme;

- a Working Group chaired by the Department of the Taoiseach and comprising of senior officials from relevant Departments has been established to identify the policy options for a financially sustainable system of long-term care, taking account of the Mercer Report on the Future Financing of Long-Term Care in Ireland and the O'Shea report on Nursing Home subventions;

- the Irish Health Services Accreditation Board has commenced work on developing accreditation standards for residential care for older people, both public and private;

- community care facilities, such as day centres for older people, have been developed by the Health Service Executive in partnership with the voluntary sector;

- an Inter-Departmental Group on the Needs of Older People was established in July 2002 primarily to examine matters which impact on the lives of older people and to ensure that a co-ordinated approach is adopted in relation to them. Up to now, it has considered issues such as housing matters and the various home improvement schemes, the information gathering process in relation to older people and the demands placed on them by that process, the consolidation and simplification of application forms, security issues and equality matters; and

- €70 million has been made available to the HSE in 2005 for the Ten Point Plan to relieve ongoing pressure on acute hospital beds and Accident and Emergency services. In relation to older people, this has meant an additional 500 patients are to receive intermediate care for up to six weeks in the private sector, 100 high dependency patients will be transferred to private nursing care and 500 additional homecare packages will be made available.

1.20 ● As part of the Health Strategy particular attention has been given to the development of a *Primary Care Strategy, Primary Care: A New Direction (2001)*. This proposed the introduction of an inter-disciplinary team-based approach (including general practitioners, nurses, home helps, paramedics and social workers) as the first point of contact that people have with the health and personal social services. This Strategy is of particular relevance to older people as it aims, for example, to develop the primary care infrastructure, reduce fragmentation, increase user participation in service planning, reduce pressure on secondary care and further develop out-of-hours services. Approval was given for the establishment of ten initial teams in October 2002, to inform the process of wider implementation (see Section 5).

1.21 ● The National Agreement *Sustaining Progress: Social Partnership Agreement 2003 – 2005* (Department of the Taoiseach, 2003) identified Care as one of ten Special Initiatives, policy areas which were considered to require a problem-solving approach to finding practical solutions. In relation to care for older people, the following priorities were identified:

- **Future financing of long-term care** – as already mentioned above, a Working Group of senior officials from relevant Departments was established to identify the policy options for a financially sustainable system of long-term care. To avoid duplication, the Project Team did not undertake a detailed analysis of this issue.

- **Pilot programme of care of older people** – Funding (€2 million in 2005) has been allocated to the Home Care Grant Scheme (see Section 3).

The International Policy Context

1.22 ● The development of policy and practice in relation to care for older people should also be considered in an international context. Current trends in this regard emphasise the importance of including older people in the policy-making process, mainstreaming ageing issues into national development frameworks and optimising older people's opportunities for social participation. There has also been a general shift towards person-centred community or home-based care and making services more consumer-friendly and standards-driven.

1.23 ● The United Nations (UN) has played a key role in the development of international policy understanding of ageing. The UN's Second World Assembly on Ageing agreed *The Madrid International Plan on Action on Ageing* in 2002. This Plan promotes an intergenerational policy approach that pays attention to all age groups with the objective of creating a society for all ages and a shift from developing policy *for* older people towards the *inclusion of* older people in the policy-making process. The UN identified three priority directions, eighteen issues, thirty-five objectives and 239 recommendations. Summary details of priorities and issues are provided in Box 1.2 overleaf. It is important to highlight that the UN commented that, at a national level, the necessary first step in the successful implementation of the Plan was to mainstream ageing and the concerns of older peoples into national development frameworks and poverty eradication strategies.

1.24 ● The World Health Organisation (2002) provides a second international policy framework for this report. In the context of global ageing, the WHO has stressed the importance of 'active ageing', the process of optimising opportunities for health, participation and security in order to enhance quality of life as people age. This approach stresses that there are eight determinants or influences that shape how individuals and populations age. Two of these determinants are cross-cutting, namely culture and gender, in that they influence the other determinants and shape responses to them. The other six determinants are:

- **HEALTH AND SOCIAL SERVICES** – health systems need to take a life course perspective that focuses on health promotion, disease prevention and equitable access to care.

- **BEHAVIOURAL** – adaptation of health lifestyles and actively participating in one's own care.

- **PERSONAL FACTORS** – biology and genetics greatly influence how a person ages.

- **PHYSICAL ENVIRONMENT** – age-friendly environments are important for all groups, but particularly for those growing older.

Box 1.2

Summary of the UN's Madrid International Plan of Action on Ageing: Priority Directions and Issues

Development

- Active participation in society and development
- Work and the ageing labour force
- Rural development, migration and urbanisation
- Access to knowledge, education and training
- Intergenerational solidarity
- Eradication of poverty
- Income security, social protection/social security and poverty prevention
- Emergency situations

Health and well-being

- Health promotion and well-being throughout life
- Universal and equal access to health-care services
- Older persons and HIV/AIDS
- Training of care providers and health professionals
- Mental health needs of older persons
- Older people and disabilities

Supportive environments for older people

- Housing and the living environment
- Care and support for caregivers
- Neglect, abuse and violence
- Images of ageing

Source: United Nations, Madrid International Plan of Action on Ageing, 2002.

- **SOCIAL ENVIRONMENT** – social support, opportunities for education and lifelong learning, peace, and protection from violence and abuse are key factors in the social environment that enhance health, participation and security as people age.

- **ECONOMIC DETERMINANTS** – this relates to three aspects in particular: income, work and social protection.

1.25 ● The WHO developed a three-pillar policy framework, guided by the UN principles of independence, participation, care, self-fulfilment and dignity. These three pillars are:

- **HEALTH** – keeping low the risk factors associated with chronic diseases and functional decline while the protective factors are kept high, and access to care for those who need it.

- **PARTICIPATION** – in socio-economic, cultural and spiritual activities, according to older people's basic human rights, capacities, needs and preferences.

- **SECURITY** – including social, financial and physical security needs and rights for people as they age to ensure protection, dignity and care when needed.

1.26 ● A third international context for the Team's work is the recently published report by the Organisation for Economic Co-operation and Development (OECD) on *Long-term Care Policies for Older People* covering 19 countries including Ireland. The OECD found that:

- there are growing expectations for better quality long-term care services at affordable costs and governments in many countries are now taking a more active role in relation to quality standards of care;

- there is a trend towards more universal public provision of long-term care services

- policies to improve the continuum of care have been achieved through a range of measures, including national strategic frameworks to outline priorities and goals and in some cases set explicit targets;

- explicit policies with the goal of shifting the balance of long-term care towards more home-based care have enabled more older people, who depend on care, to remain in their own homes; and

- cash-benefit programmes have been developed to allow dependent persons and their families more individual choice among care options. Studies have shown that greater choice and consumer direction can contribute to better quality of life at similar cost compared to traditional services. (OECD, 2005)

1.27 ● To further inform the work of the Project Team, a brief overview of the direction of policy in relation to care of older people in selected developed countries was compiled by the NESF Secretariat (Annex 4). This has highlighted a number of consistencies between countries in the way policy to address the long-term care needs of older people appears to be moving:

- There is general consensus that an ageing population requires planning and strategic responses.

- There is also considerable emphasis placed on the most appropriate way to address older people's needs, with a tendency to commit to providing services in the person's own home as much as possible. Institutional care is increasingly planned to resemble more homely environments, to encourage independence and to incorporate rehabilitation objectives.

- There is acknowledgement that the nature of informal care is changing through social and demographic change, but where it does exist it needs support.

- Care responses to needs are becoming more person-centred in both community and residential care settings.

- Co-ordinated and integrated responses to meeting the needs of older people are favoured.

- There is growing emphasis given to the need to make services more consumer-directed and standards-driven.

1.28 ● The Team recommends that a New National Strategy on Ageing should be developed by the Inter-Departmental Group on the Needs of Older People, to be chaired by the Department of the Taoiseach (see 5.11 below), to provide the strategic underpinnings for change. The Strategy should cover all service areas of relevance to older people and include consideration of the following:

- the status of older people and their contribution to society;

- baseline data and information for planning;

- current resource allocation;

- an audit of current service provision;

- cross-cutting issues such as, co-ordination, needs assessment, standards; and

- implementation, for example the value in establishing a National Office for Ageing (based on international experience and the lessons from the establishment of the National Children's Office).

Moving ahead on the Team's other recommendations does not need to be delayed until the completion of this Strategy; rather the focus should be on implementation. This Strategy should be completed by end 2006.

1.29 ● The Team now examines three over-arching issues. The first issue is the different dimensions of quality: quality of life, quality of care and quality of outcome. The second is about valuing older people's participation in society and the final issue identified here by the Team is the barriers to better community care responses.

**Different Dimensions of Quality: Quality of Life,
Quality of Care and Quality of Outcome**

1.30 ● Quality was a key principle underlying the Health Strategy *Quality and Fairness: A Health System for You*. It linked quality to two conditions:

- the development of evidence-based standards – in partnership with consumers and externally validated; and

- a situation in which continuous improvement is evaluated.

1.31 ● In relation to care for older people, three dimensions of quality can be identified. These are:

- quality of life;

- quality of care; and

- quality of outcome.

1.32 ● QUALITY OF LIFE relates to health, well-being and general life satisfaction and personal development. Good quality of life is determined by a number of factors including:

- good health, including physical functioning;

- an accessible home and community environment; and

- psychological factors, such as personality factors, the absence of loneliness and feelings of powerlessness.

The opposite (i.e. poor health, inaccessible home and communities and psychological distress) has a negative impact on quality of life, as do:

- social isolation; and

- economic deprivation (O'Shea, 2002).

A recent survey carried out for the National Council on Ageing and Older People (NCAOP) found that the quality of life and morale among older people living in the community was generally high. Over three-quarters (78 per cent) of those interviewed reported that their quality of life was good or very good (Garavan, *et al*, 2001 p.112). More recent research published by the NCAOP is consistent with this finding. It found that social networks remain strong and that the majority of older people in Ireland have a large network of family, friends and neighbours and that generally the prevalence of loneliness is low (Tracey, 2004), which indicates that older people have overall good life satisfaction.

1.33 ● Certain circumstance can reduce an individual's quality of life. While older people are not a homogeneous group, examples which may be more significant for them include:

- age – quality of life can be poorer for those over 70 years, and particularly older women;

- being single – through bereavement or not having children;

• ill-health or poor quality housing;

• worries over the availability, accessibility and cost of social care and health services;

• social exclusion and social isolation, for example due to fear of crime; and

• poverty – limiting the ability to participate in society.
  (Tracey, *et al*, 2004)

In Section 7 of our report, the Team examines how the quality of life of older people might be enhanced.

1.34 ● **QUALITY OF CARE** refers to professional standards, if possible based on evidence, by which the best outcomes are achieved, balanced against client satisfaction and organisational efficiency. Williams (1996) defined high quality care as care that is "desired by the *informed* patient or client (and family); is based on sound judgement of the professionals involved, from scientific study and/or experience; and is agreed upon and carried out in a relationship of mutual trust and respect." In this context, Garavan's (2001 p.212) finding that one in five (20 per cent) of older people did not feel that their views were significantly taken into account when they used health and social services is cause for concern. Concern regarding the quality of care in residential settings has also been raised, particularly inadequate levels of therapeutic services, insufficient focus on person-centred care, autonomy and dignity and lack of comprehensive staff training (O'Shea, 2003 pp68 – 69). We will return to the issue of quality standards in Section 7.

1.35 ● **QUALITY OF OUTCOME** refers to the impact which services have on older people and their families. There are potentially three levels to this: health and social outcomes, intermediate health outcomes and health promotion outcomes (Nutbeam, 1999). Health outcomes include the impact of care regimes and service provision on mortality, morbidity, disability and dysfunction. Social outcomes include measures such as quality of life, functional independence and equity. Intermediate health outcomes represent the determinants of these health and social outcomes, including behaviour, environment and health care services. Health promotion outcomes represent those personal, social and structural factors that can be modified in order to impact on the determinants of health. In practice, quality of outcome, therefore, has a number of defining features, including:

• strategic – with a commitment to person-centred needs, facilitating independence, empowerment and enablement;

• informed by older people themselves;

• holistic between health, housing, transport, income, etc.;

• seamless between personal, family, state, voluntary and private responses;

• equity of access based on need;

• clarity of information regarding entitlements;

- responsive and reliable (quick response to emergencies, weekend cover, etc.);

- measured and evaluated; and

- sustainable funding based on impact on quality of life.

Valuing Older People's Participation in Society

1.36 ● A fundamental premise of the Team is that every individual has something to contribute to society and this should be valued. Valuing older people's participation in society should be a given, requiring no further argument or justification. There has been some concern, however, that the projected growth in the population of older people will lead to a substantial 'burden' on finances and will be unaffordable. While it is necessary to plan for the financing of an increase in the numbers of older people, there has been a tendency for the debate to be somewhat skewed towards a negative view of ageing as increased dependency, costs and taxation for those in the active labour market.

1.37 ● To begin with, what is predicted? Projections rely on sets of assumptions and are therefore open to differences of views, but they nonetheless provide important data on likely trends. The most recent demographic projections for the period up to 2021 predict for Ireland:

- A substantial increase in the population aged 65 years and over – an increase of about 60 per cent from 436,000 in 2002 to 698,000 in 2021.

- Those 65 and over currently make up about 11 per cent of the total population – by 2021 this is projected to increase to about 15 per cent.

- Most of this growth will be among the younger old – i.e those aged 65 – 74 years.

- The trends indicate a faster growth in the population of older males compared to females; however in absolute terms older women will continue to outnumber older men.

- Apart from Dun Laoghaire-Rathdown and Waterford county, the counties projected to have the highest percentage of older people in twenty years time are in the western half of the country – that said, a quarter of all older people are projected to live in Dublin city and county.

- There will be a shift towards married and separated older people and, in general, a shift away from single and widowed.

- The numbers of those living alone will increase largely in line with the general growth in the numbers of older people – but this will represent a substantial absolute increase from 114,00 in 2002 to 210,000 in 2021. The number of those aged 70 and over living alone is projected to almost double – from 88,400 in 2002 to 161,900 in 2021.

- While the projections above predict a substantial increase in the number of older people, due to changes in the overall population structure, the ratio of dependent people (i.e. those aged below 15 and over 65) to those considered of working age (15-64 years) is predicted to increase only

moderately over the next two decades and Ireland will continue to have a low dependency ratio by international standards.
(Connell and Pringle, 2004)

1.38 ● Beyond 2021, the population is projected to continue to rise; the *UN World Population Prospects* predicts that the population of Ireland will reach 5.762 million by the year 2050. As Graph 1.1 (below) shows, by the middle of this Century over a quarter (25.9 per cent) of the Irish population will be aged 65 and over, but this remains below the EU 25 average of almost 30 per cent aged 65 and over.

1.39 ● Valuing older people's participation in society is a core theme of this report. In Figure 1.1 opposite the different influences on older people's

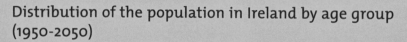

Graph 1.1 Population Projections by Age Group, Ireland and EU 25

Distribution of the population in Ireland by age group (1950-2050)

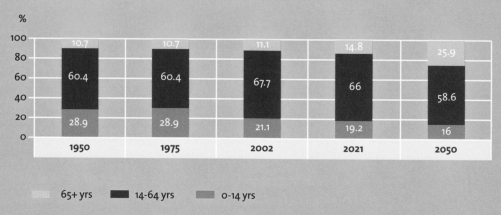

Age distribution of the population in EU 25 by age group (1950-2050)

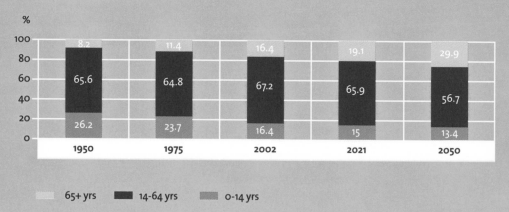

Source: UN World Population Prospects (2004 Revision) and Connell, P & Pringle, D, 2004.
Population Ageing in Ireland: Projections 2002-2021, Dublin: NCAOP.

participation are clustered under four headings:

• adding years to life and life to years;

• social inclusion and representation;

• person-centred, holistic and integrated services; and

• enabling environments.

These will have differing meanings and impacts for each individual, which serves to emphasise the importance of consulting with older people collectively (and individually in the context of their personal care plans) regarding their needs and preferences. Valuing older people's participation in society relies, however, on these four different but inter-dependent aspects being acknowledged at both strategic and service delivery levels, and by policy-makers, services providers and users and society generally.

Each of these four areas is now examined in turn.

Figure 1.1 Influences on Older People's Participation in Society

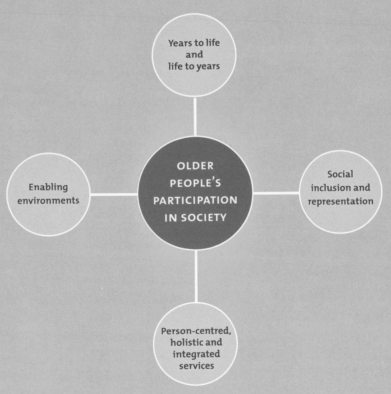

Years to life and life to years

1.40 ● The most obvious determinant of participation in society for older people is their life expectancy, and in this regard, older people here do not fare well compared to the European Union average. Table 1.3 below compares the life expectancy for males and females and shows that for both sexes Irish life expectancy is generally below the average, particularly for those aged 65 and over. Life expectancy at birth has increased by roughly 2 years over this ten year period for both men and women in Ireland. Life expectancy for women continues to outpace that of men. Over the last ten years, however, the life expectancy at birth gap between women and men has shortened slightly from 5.5 years to 5.1 years.

Table 1.3 Life Expectancy at Birth and at Age 65 (years)

i) Life Expectancy at Birth (years)

	Female		Male	
	1992	2002	1992	2002
EU 25	79.1	81.1	72.2	74.8
EU 15	79.9	81.6	73.3	75.8
Ireland	78.2	80.3	72.7	75.2

ii) Life Expectancy at age 65 (years)

	Female		Male	
	1992	2002	1992	2002
EU 25	...	19.6	...	16.0
EU 15	18.8	19.9	15.0	16.3
Ireland	17.2	18.6	13.5	15.3

Source: Eurostat.

1.41 ● A second determinant of older people's participation in society is healthy life expectancy, as time spent in poor health in later years is very likely to impact negatively on social participation. On this measure also, Ireland does not score well in international comparisons. In a ranking of 23 developed countries, the Word Health Organisation showed Irish males second last and Irish females last. The gap between Ireland and the best performing country (Japan) for healthy life expectancy is 3.2 years for males and 4.6 years for females.

1.42 ● We will return to examine this issue in more detail (Section 7). Here however it is important to flag the crucial role which life-long health promotion can play in supporting older people's participation in society.

Social Inclusion and Representation

1.43 ● Inadequate income and resources (material, cultural and social) place some older people at risk of exclusion and marginalisation from participating in activities which are considered the norm for other people in society. This risk needs to be acknowledged and addressed. The majority of older people manage to avoid the extremes of deprivation, *even given that they have low incomes,* due to a combination of factors such as the impact of non-cash benefits (free travel, medical card, etc) the accumulation of resources over time and lower patterns of consumption and levels of expectation (Layte, *et al,* 1999). The findings from recent national poverty surveys are presented in Table 1.4 below and show that older people tend to have a slightly lower than average risk of consistent poverty (that is low income and lacking items generally considered necessary). Women, particularly those living alone (especially in rural areas), were found to be at particular risk. During the period 1998 – 2001, a downward trend in the proportion of those consistently poor is evident.

Table 1.4 Trends in Consistent Poverty 1998 – 2003

	1998 (%)	2000 (%)	2001 (%)	2003(%)*
Older People	6.6	5.9	3.9	7.0
All Age Groups	8.2	6.2	5.2	9.4

Sources 1998 – 2001 Living in Ireland Survey (LIIS), 2003 EU-Survey on Income and Living Conditions (EU SILC).
*Note: The EU-SILC replaced the LIIS in 2003 and the consistent poverty rates between the two surveys are not comparable.

1.44 ● The figures for 2003 are not directly comparable to those from earlier years, due to a change in survey methodology (Central Statistics Office, 2005). But it is clear that the National Anti-Poverty Strategy target: *"Over the period to 2007, aim to reduce the numbers of those who are 'consistently poor' below 2 per cent and, if possible, eliminate consistent poverty"* is now impossible to achieve.

1.45 ● The income of older people is significantly reduced by their lower rates of labour force participate, compared to younger age groups. Income is important in facilitating people of all ages to participate in society. Participation in the labour market is a key source of income, but labour force participation among older age groups has generally been lower than those of younger age groups. It is important that pensions are both adequate and sustainable, and are part of a broader strategy to reduce the high risk of poverty faced by many of those in retirement (National Economic and Social Council, 2005).

1.46 ● Particular groups of older people may be at greater risk of social exclusion due to additional circumstances or cumulative disadvantage. Examples under this heading include: those with dementia, an intellectual disability, the homeless or those with experience of elder abuse. We return to examine this issue in more detail in Section 6 of the report.

1.47 ● A second point here is the representation of older people in society and the role which this plays in their social participation. In a recent survey of attitudes to ageing and older people (Hodgins and Greve, 2004) high proportions of the general population (and of older people themselves) felt that older people make a positive contribution to society and that they should be included in groups that decide on local or national policy.

1.48 ● The interests of older people are represented by a number of voluntary and statutory bodies, as detailed in Box 1.3 below. A number of national organisations, such as the Alzheimer Society of Ireland and the Carers' Association, also have strong links with the interest of older people. In addition, there are, as reflected in the large number of written submissions received by the Project Team (see Annex 3), a substantial number of locally-based organisations with views on the barriers to the greater participation of older people in society and an interest in influencing policy developments.

Box 1.3

Main National Organisations Representing the Specific Interests of Older People

Statutory	■ National Council on Ageing and Older People
Voluntary	■ Age Action Ireland
	■ Age and Opportunity
	■ ALONE
	■ Federation of Active Retirement Associations
	■ Irish Senior Citizens Parliament
	■ Older Women's Network
	■ The Irish Association of Older People

1.49 ● It is important that the voice of older people is included in planning and development at a national and local level. This involves investing in the capacity of older people and older people's organisations to be involved, for example through training, and also that local and national bodies actively consult with and involve older people in planning which affects them (see Section 5). Equally, it is important that service providers establish customer groups and resident committees as feedback mechanisms, for example in sheltered housing schemes, nursing homes, day care centres, etc., and that these customer groups are actively supported to develop their capacity to have a say on services which impact on their lives.

Person-centred, holistic and integrated services

1.50 ● This is another theme running through this report - one that is familiar to the policy debate on older people over the last twenty years at least. Person-centred, holistic and integrated services are important determining factors in everyone's participation in society. For some older people they may be particularly important, especially those who are cash poor and may rely more than others on public services to address their needs and who may not be in a position to access alternative services.

1.51 ● The requirement for person-centred, holistic and integrated services has been acknowledged for some time now and some progress has been made at the level of pilot projects and special initiatives. But the Team identifies this as a particular area in need of further significant improvement, at the strategic, service planning and service delivery levels (see Section 3).

Enabling Environments

1.52 ● Ageist attitudes in society, setting limits on what older people can and cannot do, sometimes stop them from participating fully in economic and social life. The Team examines this issue in more detail in Section 2 of the report but here it is important to stress that overcoming these attitudes within society is the first step in achieving better levels of participation. Public policy must challenge ageism and ageist behaviour through effective legislation, regulation and on-going monitoring and review.

1.53 ● Other aspects of enabling environments are also examined throughout this report, including:

- **HOUSING** – good housing enables older people to continue living independently and to maintain life-time social contacts and networks.

- **TRANSPORT** – to encourage and support social integration and to facilitate access to community care services, such as day care.

- **PHYSICAL AND ENVIRONMENTAL DESIGN** – good environmental design can support older people's participation in society, especially when it is linked to consumer preferences and empowerment.

- **SAFETY AND SECURITY** – here, perceptions of safety can be as important as actual experiences.

- **ENABLING TECHNOLOGY** – this has considerable potential to facilitate greater social participation in society. A number of written submissions to the Team drew attention to the valuable role which telecare services and assistive technology can play in maintaining independence, reducing fear and isolation, managing risks (for example, from dementia, strokes and falls; as well as physical risks such as intruders and fires or floods), medication management and compliance and facilitating early discharge from hospital.

Barriers to Achieving Better Community Care

1.54 ● There is no legal definition in Irish legislation of what constitutes 'community care' and a lack of clarity on service eligibility (see Section 4). As part of the services for older people, community care generally means helping people who need care and support to live with dignity and independence in the community, usually in the person's own home or the home of a relative. But it could also include care provided in specially provided facilities within the local community, for example in some form of sheltered or supported housing with varying degrees of supervision and /or nursing care. The care involved may be provided by a combination of sources: family members or voluntary carers, public health nursing, home help, day centres, paramedical services such as occupational therapy and chiropody, meals on wheels, etc. Community care is often seen in contrast to institutional care. This is usually provided in long-stay care places such as welfare homes, geriatric units, district hospitals and in private nursing homes. It is not useful, however, to consider these as two separate and unrelated entities; rather it is more appropriate to consider them as a continuum, along which people may move over and back depending on their particular needs at a particular time.

1.55 ● Defining community care in terms of helping people to remain in their own communities in dignity and independence broadens the parameters of 'community care' beyond purely health and personal social services to incorporate a wide range of other services including income maintenance, housing, transport and life-long learning. It also means that 'community care' is less about the physical location of the service recipient and more about the philosophical under-pinning of the services provided and the approach adopted. In this way, it is not a contradiction to provide community-care services in locally-based long-stay situations, particularly if the objective of the service is rehabilitation towards more independent living.

1.56 ● Many families play a crucial role in supporting older people who wish to remain living at home or in their community to do so. In the written submissions received and in our consultations with various groups, the role of carers has been raised repeatedly and the Team fully endorses the view that carers should be more fully supported (see Section 3).

1.57 ● *The Years Ahead* (1988, p.39) proposed that services for older people should be:

- comprehensive
- equitable
- accessible
- responsive
- flexible
- co-ordinated
- planned
- cost-effective

These are still useful starting points for considering community-care and how it should respond to people's needs. We currently lack more modern guiding principles of community care, however, which are necessary to inform and underpin a strategic vision of ageing in a community setting and make it a reality for older people to live in greater dignity in their own homes.

1.58 ● Guiding Principles of Community Care developed in Australia are presented in Box 1.4 overleaf as a potential model. They place emphasis on the support of family carers, the need for clarity regarding access to services, the value of responsive and planned services, the assessment of needs, equity, financial sustainability, information and quality. The development of guiding principles for Ireland, however, requires consultation with the many stakeholders, including older people and their families, service providers, policy-makers and the general public.

Box 1.4

Guiding Principles of Community Care in Australia

- Family carers are crucial to any community care system and require support in their caring role;

- Access to community care services needs to be clear and straightforward;

- The service delivery system should be person-focused and responsive to the needs of individuals;

- Case orientation and management of services is most important and cost-effective for those care recipients with very high level or complex needs;

- Appropriate care is underpinned by appropriate assessment;

- A consistent and sustainable mix of community care services should be accessible for care recipients and carers from all geographical regions;

- The care system should be financially sustainable;

- Information flows must support continuity of care and minimise duplication in information gathering; and

- People using community care services should be assured of quality services.

Source: Commonwealth Department of Health and Ageing (2003)

1.59 ● There is much to commend in the current system of care for older people. Through the Team's visits to different care settings, by talking to older people, their carers and experts and in the written submissions received, examples of good practice, innovation and the potential for improvement were evident. But it is clear that improvements are necessary if older people's preferences and indeed official policy are to be realised. In its discussions and deliberations, the Team has identified the following barriers to the development of better community care services in this country:

- **THE LEGAL UNDERPINNING OF COMMUNITY CARE IS WEAK** – the lack of a legal basis for community care and, in contrast, the more advanced legal underpinning of policy in relation to children and institutional care for older people ultimately limits the choices open to service providers and older people themselves.

- **SERVICES FOLLOW FUNDING** – while the overall level of funding in care for older people has increased in recent years, its allocation still favours medically-based and institutional responses, with the larger proportion of current programme funding going to residential compared to community-based care (see Table 1.2 p.6).

- **RESIDENTIAL CARE BIAS** – financial supports and incentives favour long-stay care over community-based care.

- **AN AGE-FRIENDLY APPROACH IS UNDERDEVELOPED** – the mindset underpinning policy development and implementation needs to give greater value to ageing and older people in our society. Ageism attitudes inhibit the development of innovative approaches and access on the basis of need.

- **CO-ORDINATION AND INTEGRATED RESPONSES ARE LACKING** – at both national and local levels and within services (e.g. institutional and community services) between different social services (health and personal social services, housing, transport, etc) and different providers – public, private and voluntary. Services do not sufficiently place the individual at the centre, rather the traditional approach is one where the older person is expected to 'fit' themselves into the services which are available, and this is a barrier to progress.

- **STANDARDS ARE UNCLEAR** – there is a lack of clarity on what a good community care service is, what older people should expect and what should be expected from service providers. Some standards are laid down in law in relation to institutional care, but these are not applied equally in all settings. The development of clearer standards is, therefore, a first step to achieving quality outcomes.

- **CARE RESPONSES ARE CRISIS DRIVEN, INFLEXIBLE AND TOO SLOW** – the majority of older people lead very independent lives and may only come into contact with care services following a crisis, such as the onset of an illness or following an accident or alternatively their care needs may increase gradually over a number of years. Community support services need to be more proactive in trying to prevent dependency arising in the first place and when care needs do arise they should be in a position to respond quickly and comprehensively with the objective of restoring the person to independence as soon as possible, if that is their wish.

- **SERVICES ARE PATCHY** – older people in different parts of the country should be able to access a range of primary care services on an equitable basis, and this is not always the case. Difficulties in relation to staff recruitment, staff shortages (e.g. paramedical staff) and the need for staff training and re-training delay response times. The varying nature of services also makes it difficult for older people to find out what is available in their area. Equal access to core services across the country is required. Similarly, the supports for those in need of hospice and palliative care services in both community and institutional settings is uneven around the country and inadequate to meet needs.

- **COVERAGE TIME OF SERVICES IS TOO RESTRICTED** – community services are not adequately responding to the 'out-of-core office hours' nature of some older people's needs. Absence of community care services during the evening, at weekends, over holidays periods, etc., is a substantial barrier to the development of services. This will have implications for both staffing levels and work practices.

- **Shortage of community-based staff** – shortages in the supply of community-based chiropodists, community social work services and physiotherapists were identified in particular.

- **Lack of evidence-based policy development and service delivery** – data collection and collation in relation to individual and group needs is in need of improvement and many of the services provided are not regularly evaluated to see how well they are performing to meet overall policy objectives. Medical data could also be better used to plan services.

- **Insufficient consultation with older people and their carers** – the large number of written submissions received by the Project Team from older people is just one testament to the value of their input at a general policy level. They also need to be more involved in their own care planning, with needs assessment linked to appropriately trained staff.

- **Weakness of representation and advocacy** – while there are a number of organisations representing the interests of older people (Box 1.3), there is a lack of co-ordination between groups and older people do not have a strong 'customer' voice. The lack of advocacy for vulnerable older people is an additional weakness.

- **A lack of clarity regarding the balance of responsibility for caring** – the Mercer Report (2002) acknowledged that there are diverging views on who should be responsible for long-term care – the individual, the family or the State. Also, the nature of informal care may change in future as a result of falling birth rates and greater participation of women in the labour market. Ultimately, it is society's values which determine policy and financial priorities, and the lack of public debate and clarity on the respective caring roles and responsibilities of the family and the State limit the development of policy in this area.

1.60   ● This is a challenging set of barriers to be addressed and a strategic response needs to be drawn up, prioritised and implemented over a number of years. The lack of an overall strategic policy vision of what it should mean to be ageing in Irish society is an overarching barrier in trying to address these problems (see para. 1.23 above). Furthermore, the policy commitments that do exist, such as those in the Health Strategy *Quality and Fairness: A Health System for You and The Years Ahead,* have met with very limited progress towards implementation to-date.

1.61 ● Greatest urgency is now required for change. Care for older people lacks a strategic vision and a comprehensive and modern implementation plan. While the majority of older people manage to live independent lives in their own communities, more integrated and person-centred service responses could enhance older people's independence, dignity and choice. The population is ageing, with the numbers aged 65 and over predicted to grow by as much as 60 per cent by 2021. Due to changes in the population structure, however, the overall dependency levels are predicted to increase only moderately over the next two decades and we will continue to have a low dependency ratio by international standards (Pringle, 2004). Projected demographic change cannot, therefore, be regarded as a reason for postponing improved care arrangements for older people.

1.62 ● As outlined above, our recent economic growth provides the potential for higher spending on services for older people. Encouraging and facilitating people to save for their older age to insure they have adequate pensions and savings to access some of the services they require is equally important. The potential role which technology can play in improving the quality of older people's lives should not be underestimated.

Structure of the Report

1.63 ● In the next Section, the Team examines the issue of ageism, which must be addressed if progress is to be made. The elements of making living at home in old age possible are examined in Section 3. The focus of Section 4 is legal aspects of community care and this is followed by Section 5, which concentrates on overcoming the barriers to co-ordination. In keeping with the NESF's particular mandate to focus on those most marginalised, issues relating to vulnerable older people are examined in Section 6. Enhancing quality of care and quality of life are discussed in Section 7 and then in Section 8 the focus shifts to delivering the required changes and achieving implementation.

Introduction

2.1 ● A central argument in this report is that ageism and age discrimination are an unwelcome reality in our society. This discrimination inhibits older people's full and dignified social participation. Responsibility for tackling ageism rests with all sections of society. While there have been some efforts to counteract age discrimination and ageism, further concrete actions are required to address its causes and consequences. As a starting principle, the application of age limits should not in any way disadvantage older people.

What is Ageism?

2.2 ● Ageism can impact on anybody at any time in their life. In relation to older people, it refers to deep-rooted negative beliefs about older people and the ageing process, which may then give rise to different types of age discrimination. These views are created and reinforced by society, and are reflected in everyday norms of behaviour. The term 'ageism' was coined by Robert Butler in the late 1960s when he defined it as 'a process of systematic stereotyping and discrimination against people because of their chronological age' (Butler, 1969). He identified three main aspects to ageism:

• prejudicial attitudes towards older people, old age and the ageing process;

• discriminatory practices against older people; and

• institutional practices and policies that fuel stereotypes about older people.

2.3 ● Stereotypes play a central role in framing ageism, as they define role expectations and undermine a person's individuality. Stereotypes of older people include:

• older people are 'all the same';

• older people are rigid, frail, disabled, stuck in their ways, even confused; and

• older people are lonely and isolated.

These stereotypes lead to prejudicial attitudes, which are typically negative and hostile. There is a high risk of age discrimination 'when someone makes or sees a distinction because of another person's age and uses that as a basis for unfair treatment of that person'. Such discrimination can be direct – such as upper age limits on access to services – and indirect – such as a lower quality of service for older people or where care is provided in such a way that the outcomes are less favourable for older people. These negative stereotypes can have very real consequences for older people, damaging self-image, finances, relationships and mental health. According to one long-term study, older people with positive perceptions of ageing lived longer than those with negative images (cited in Huber, 2005 p.2).

2.4 ● Another way to consider discrimination is to distinguish between positive and negative discrimination. In some circumstances, older people in Irish society are treated more favourably than other groups because of their age (see Box 2.1 opposite). There are arguments to support positive discrimination – it helps to counteract negative discrimination, it facilitates older people to participate in society more fully and acts as an anti-poverty measure. The Equal Status Acts 2000 – 2004 allow preferential treatment or the taking of positive measures to either promote equality of opportunity for disadvantaged people or to cater for a person's special needs.

2.5 ● Negative discrimination, on the other hand, is not justifiable. For example, women aged 65 and over are not able to access Breastcheck, a free breast X-ray screening programme, even though the chances of developing breast cancer increase with age. The National Cancer Registry (2005) found that for the years 1994 – 2001 treatment rates fell for almost all cancers with increasing age at diagnosis, although it is not clear why this is the case. Similarly those who develop a disability aged over 65 are not included in the Physical and Sensory Disability Database, even though there is no upper age limit for inclusion on the Intellectual Disability Database and 42 per cent of people with disabilities are aged over 65. Examples of positive and negative discrimination are given in Box 2.1 opposite.

Box 2.1

Older People: Examples of Positive and Negative Discrimination

Positive

- Free Travel Pass

- Medical Card for all those aged over 70, regardless of means

- Fuel and electricity allowances and free telephone rental for those living alone

- Grants scheme to improve the security of older people (Community Support for Older People scheme)

- Age Tax Credit for those aged 65 years and over

- Free passports for those 65 years and over

- Housing grants for essential repairs

Negative

- Upper age limit for inclusion in the Physical and Sensory Disability Database

- Regional variations in access to stroke rehabilitation, cardiac service, intensive care and oncology services (McGlone, *et al*, 2005)

- Personal Assistant services available to disabled people, not offered to people aged over 65

- Disability Act, 2005 – allows for phased implementation for different age groups

- Upper Age limit (70 years) applies to membership of Institute of Technology Governing Bodies

Prevalence of Ageism in Policy and Practice

2.6 ● Recent studies indicate that ageist attitudes to older people in Ireland are not uncommon and that these attitudes may have negative consequences for older people's quality of life and access to services:

• Negative attitudes to older people was raised in the public consultations regarding the Health Strategy *Quality and Fairness — a Health System for You*. A typical quote from the consultations was:

"The elderly are treated as though they should be grateful for any treatment given to them even when this undermines their dignity and privacy. At times, the elderly are treated like children or as though they are intellectually impaired. For example, treatment, tests, results, diagnoses etc are not given to them so that they are in a state of fear as to what is actually wrong with them and what will happen to them. In my experience, only some health professionals will actually talk to the elderly" (Department of Health and Children, 2002, p.46).

• In a survey of 543 older people, over half (54 per cent) reported that they experienced ageism, 40 per cent of the incidences were reported to have occurred 'more than once' (Stokes, *et al*, 2003).

• In a survey of the general population on attitudes to older people and their ageing, over one third (36 per cent) of respondents thought that older people (defined as people in their fifties and over) were treated worse than the general population because of their age, although it is interesting to note that fewer of those aged 70 years and over expressed this view (21 per cent) (O'Connor and Dowds, 2005).

• Allegations of discrimination on the age ground make up 10 per cent of the case files of the Equality Authority under the Employment Equality Act and 9 per cent of the case files under the Equal Status Act (Crowley, 2005).

2.7 ● The experience of ageism at a national and societal level is also reflected in policy and practices around service delivery. A recent qualitative study of ageism within the health services (McGlone, 2005), which involved consultation with over 450 older people and 150 health service staff, reported a considerable level of institutionalised ageism:

• Many older people consulted said they felt 'fobbed off' because of their age;

• Staff also felt that older people were treated differently because of their age, for instance they were not being referred on to specialist services;

• Indirect discrimination was identified – for instance staff reported that acute cases (those that can be healed) were favoured over chronic cases (those requiring maintenance and relief of symptoms), the latter are more commonly associated with older age;

• Staff also identified barriers to accessing services which were more likely to adversely affect older people, for instance, explicit and implicit age limits on services, geographical location, excess bureaucracy and possession of a medical card;

• Lack of transport, long waiting lists to access services and long waits in Accident and Emergency Departments and Out-Patient clinics were also raised by older people as barriers to services. While these are issues which can be considered to affect people of all ages, they can have particular and more severe consequences for older people;

• Staff also pointed to the limited availability of services for older people, such as social workers, occupational therapy, speech and language therapy, chiropody and physiotherapy, health screening, mental health services, access to equipment and aids, due to a lack of staff and resources;

• Deficiencies in the level of community supports, such as Public Health Nurses, were also identified by health service staff and the lack of these supports was considered to contribute to delays in hospital discharges. Older people themselves reported that the lack of community supports limited their choice to live independently; and

• Staff reported significant improvements on the approach to care of older people, but a degree of stereotyping older people as 'less capable' and as 'bed-blockers' persisted (McGlone, 2005).

2.8 ● These research findings relate to health services, but it is likely that ageism has also percolated the planning and delivery of many services. This is a serious and persistent problem and one that requires concentrated attention if older people are to continue living as independently as possible for as long as possible. What is required here is a concerted mind-shift from society, policy makers and planners, service deliverers and users. The observation made in a written submission to the Project Team from a voluntary organisation which provides age awareness training to policy makers and health care workers indicates the scale of the task involved:

"Even when much goodwill is in evidence towards the older people with whom they work (i.e. the course participants), it can be expressed in quite disempowering terms with insufficient awareness of older people as active participants in their own care or of their right to continue to shape their own futures, let alone of people who still have a contribution to make to society generally" (written submission).

2.9 ● As a concrete starting point, age alone should not be the deciding factor when decisions are being made regarding access to and availability of services, but rather these decisions should be made on the basis of needs and ability to benefit. Some models of service delivery have a tradition of being age-related, such as day care centres and special wards. The assumption that older people prefer this model of care needs to be supported by evidence. Alternative models are needed for those with different preferences. Indeed, relating responses to need rather than age does not necessarily mean that there is no place for age-related services. It is important that services are able to respond to the complex needs of some older people, and in some cases, this may best be achieved in 'age-related care settings'. It is equally important, however, that when older people are in age-related care settings that this does not disadvantage them in any way.

Addressing Ageism at a Personal and Policy Level

2.10 ● Addressing ageism involves considering it at both the institutional and the personal level. At the institutional level, removing age barriers and unnecessary age-segregation are key; while at a personal level becoming more aware of the impact which stereotyped attitudes can have on the quality of relationships a person might have with another is important. Bytheway (1995, p.126) points out that ageing is a shared experience, that we are all subject to ageism, and he emphasises that if we are to address ageism the ideology and cultural division between 'us' and 'them' must be tackled. We should be celebrating longevity as it is in all our own personal best interests.

2.11 ● Considerable effort is already being made to highlight the negative
consequences of age discrimination and to counteract ageism. For example:

• Age is included as one of the Nine Grounds in our equality legislation
(see NESF, 2002).

• The 'Say no to Ageism Week', jointly organised by the Health Service
Executive, the Equality Authority and the National Council on Ageing and
Older People now takes place in May of each year.

• Organisations representing the interests of older people have designed
and implemented age equality awareness training.

2.12 ● It is clear, however, that these actions need to be built on and advanced
if ageism is to be more fully addressed. Box 2.2 opposite outlines the
approach which the Team recommends in tackling this problem. These
actions need to be informed by a *Government level statement* that age
discrimination and ageism are unacceptable realities of the current system
and ones which there is a commitment to eliminate. It is also important
that issues relating to ageism and older people are not treated in isolation,
but that they are embedded in broader strategies, such as the National
Development Plan, to achieve social integration and intergenerational
solidarity.

2.13 ● A driving force is required to move from this broad aspiration to more
tangible actions in line with the recommendations of the NCAOP
(McGlone, *et al*, 2005). This requires the establishment of a Working
Group on Positive Ageing by the Department of Health and Children,
which would be tasked with:

• commissioning an independent audit of existing policies and procedures
in each Government Department and public body to identify ageist
practices;

• developing a strategy to address any practices identified;

• consulting with older people and their families and representative groups;

• promoting positive ageing in both the private and public sectors, which
would build on the model of the National Children's Office;

• developing anti-ageism guidelines and advising on how future policies
should be age-proofed to avoid further ageism; and

• monitoring progress and producing an annual report.

Box 2.2

Strategy to Root out Ageism and to Promote Positive Ageing

The Team recommends that a National Strategy to Root out Ageism and Promote Positive Ageing should be developed at three inter-connecting levels.

At **Government level**, a Statement that ageism and age discrimination should be eliminated should be published. The promotion of an age-friendly society should be mainstreamed in national strategies (e.g the National Development Programme). These are immediate priorities.

At the **Policy level** a Working Group on Positive Ageing should be established by the Department of Health and Children on publication of the Team's report. It should have a broad membership of Government Departments, Social Partners and experts to:

- audit existing Departmental policy and procedures and develop a strategic response;
- consult with older people and others;
- promote positive ageing in both the public and private sectors;
- develop national anti-ageism guidelines and advise on age-proofing; and
- monitor progress and produce an annual report.

This should be linked to the **Delivery level**, where relevant statutory service providers, for example, the Health Service Executive and Local Authorities, should pay greater attention to the needs of older people through:

- better inter-agency liaison at a senior level on positive ageing issues;
- the inclusion of age equality as a cross-cutting theme in strategic planning;
- age-proofing and auditing services from an age impact perspective and using administrative data to check for age discrimination;
- raising public awareness of ageism issues;
- including older people in customer groups;
- staff training; and
- supporting local initiatives.

In addition, the County and City Development Boards should develop positive ageing approaches. Progress should be reported to the National Working Group on Positive Ageing.

Source : Department of Health and Children (2001) Quality and Fairness: A Health System for You. p.150-151.

2.14 ● The Team recommends that the Department of Health and Children should take the lead in convening and offering the Secretariat to this Group but, in recognising that ageing is not a disease, it may be appropriate for another Department or agency to chair the group. The Group's Membership should include the Departments of: the Taoiseach; the Environment, Heritage and Local Government; Social and Family Affairs; Community, Rural and Gaeltacht Affairs; Justice Equality and Law Reform; Education and Science; Arts, Sport and Tourism; and Transport. This group should operate in the context of the Social Partnership Agreement and include the Social Partners and additional experts.

2.15 ● It is generally acknowledged that the elimination of ageism is a long-term goal and it is important therefore that the Group should produce an annual report which would chart progress and offer advice on future priorities.

2.16 ● Actions are also required at the service delivery level. Here, the Team recommends that:

• a lead role should be taken by the relevant statutory service providers, for example, the Health Service Executive and the Local Authorities, to pay greater attention to the needs of older people such as:

• senior officers in both the HSE and the Local Authorities should be responsible for liaison on positive ageing issues;

• local level strategic planning to include age equality as cross-cutting theme;

• age impact assessments to be undertaken to test policies and services at design stage for their impact on equality for older people and an audit of local services should be undertaken to identify any ageist practices, procedures and perceptions and necessary actions taken;

• public ageism and age discrimination awareness to be raised;

• services to be audited for age discrimination practices;

• consumer user groups to be established and to include older people;

• age awareness training for staff;

• local level initiatives and innovation should be encouraged and supported;

• the County and City Development Boards should develop positive ageing approaches;

• a data strategy to use administrative data to gather information on services to assess any direct or indirect age discrimination should be devised and implemented; and

• progress should be reported to the National Working Group on Positive Ageing.

Realising the Potential of all Older People

2.17 ● The Team has focused in particular on ageism as it represents a substantial barrier to implementing the policies necessary to move towards better care for older people. Realising the potential of all older people is at the core of the Team's approach. This means striving towards a more age-friendly society, one which welcomes and celebrates the projected increase in the number of older people as a success rather than as a 'problem' or 'challenge' and seeks to harness this (see National Council on Ageing and Older People, 2005).

2.18 ● It should also be remembered that the projected increase in the proportion of the population over 65 years of age is likely to level-off from 2050 (at around 30 per cent of the total population) and while we are facing age-related fiscal challenges, analysts predict that we are in a good position to deal with these (Barrett and Bergin, 2005). Mullen (2002) challenges the idea that ageing is a major economic and social burden and argues that even quite low levels of economic growth will be sufficient to satisfy even the most extreme projections on the future pace of ageing. For example, he argues that there is no connection between ageing and increased health care costs or indeed between demography and economic growth.

2.19 ● Finally, it is important to stress again that a high degree of old age dependency is socially conditioned and created, through labour market practices, through approaches to service provision, through a lack of older people's involvement in decision-making, through the lack of holistic approaches to needs assessment and through delayed and inappropriate interventions. It is also reinforced by media coverage and images of ageing and the ageing process, which all too often stereotype older people as dependent. In the next Section of the Report, the Team examines the changes necessary to make independent living at home more possible.

Introduction

3.1 ● Making living at home possible for as many older people as possible is a core policy objective of this report and the preferred choice of older people themselves. In this Section, the Team considers how this might be achieved by extending the choices available to older people, supporting their independence and empowerment, developing flexible responses to needs and supporting carers who are often older people as well.

Choice, Autonomy and Empowerment

3.2 ● From the Team's consultations and in the written submissions received, a common theme that emerged was that services are not sufficiently tailored around the individual; on the contrary, often older people have to fit in with what is available in their area and, if the service they need is not available, they have to go without. A 'one size fits all' approach is not, however, appropriate in supporting independence and autonomy; rather, tailored services are needed to reflect people's different circumstances and preferences.

3.3 ● Box 3.1 overleaf, sets out a set of principles proposed by the Project Team to achieve a better service delivery for older people. The underlying aim here is to put the service user at the centre of the service. It recognises the value of early intervention, and the importance of moving away from the current model where an older person often gets help only when they have reached a crisis point; and moving forward to a model where services are flexible, timely and barriers to access are actively addressed. The promotion of independence and well-being should be core to service delivery and this can only be achieved where services are customer-centred, respectful and transparent. It is also important that services shift to a stronger focus on better outcomes for older people, and that these are measured on an on-going basis. A key factor to secure the necessary changes in all of this is providing leadership to drive the implementation process forward, and the Team returns to this issue in Section 8 of the report.

Box 3.1

Principles of Better Service Delivery

Principles	Delivery
▪ Available, affordable and timely	▪ A range of services should be available to all older people in an equitable way that recognise and respond to their varying needs and means in a timely fashion. A range of regulated service providers (State, voluntary, community and private) is needed to promote choice.
▪ Comprehensive, multi-disciplinary and integrated	▪ Services should be comprehensive, multi-disciplinary and well resourced; integrated *within* services, e.g. primary and second-ary health levels and *between* sectors, health, housing, etc.
▪ Flexible at point of delivery	▪ Barriers to accessing services should be actively removed. For example, opening hours, locations, transport, mobility and caring issues need to be considered in a flexible and holistic way. Where possible, a single point of contact to access services should be developed.
▪ Localised	▪ Services should be able to respond to local needs, in planning and delivery, and be informed by consultation with older people and local service providers.
▪ Promote independence and well-being	▪ Services should be preventative in approach, accessible early to promote independence and well-being and halt avoidable dependency and crisis-led interventions.
▪ Respectful and transparent	▪ Services should be customer-centred; centred on dignity, choice and independence, with quality standard measurements and clear regulation.
▪ Outcome driven	▪ Services for older people need to have as their core purpose better outcomes for older people (including as older people themselves define it) and these should be measured on an on-going basis.
▪ Leadership	▪ Political and organisational leadership is needed to drive implementation.

3.4 ● These principles lead to a more person-centred approach to service delivery, which puts the older person at the core. In Figure 3.1 opposite, this is presented as an organisational chart with all of the aspects which make living at home for as long as possible feeding into the centre. Greater choice, autonomy and empowerment for older people involve not just the provision of health services but a coming together of all the relevant facets of active ageing. Box 3.2 below gives an example of a person-centred model of care operating in the North Western Region.

3.5 ● The Team address these issues individually and collectively throughout the report. Here two areas, housing and transport, which were flagged in the consultation process as key enablers to facilitate older people to remain living in their own homes for longer, are examined in more detail.

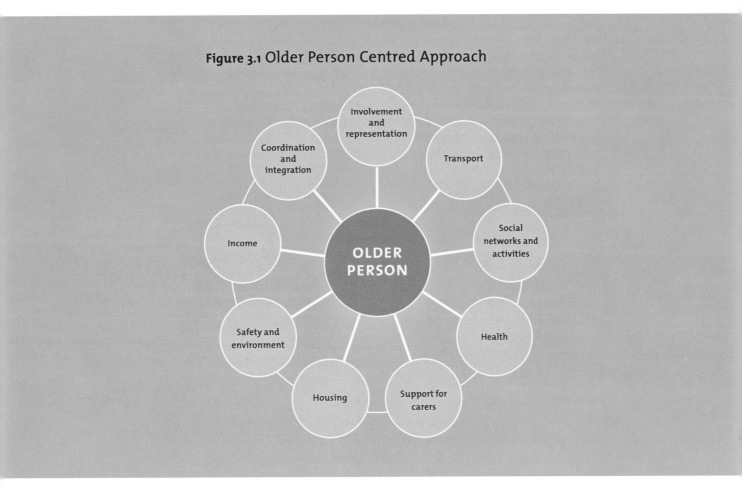

Figure 3.1 Older Person Centred Approach

Housing and Transport as Key Enablers

Housing

3.6 ● Housing is a very important issue for many older people, not just as a form of shelter, but as a grounding of community connections, networks and supports which have been built up over a lifetime. Housing can, however, be a considerable worry to maintain and to adapt to changing levels of health and mobility. In excess of 80 per cent of older householders own their homes outright (Watson and Williams, 2003), and for this group their housing can be a considerable asset, and one which has the potential to afford people greater choice, empowerment and independence.

Box 3.2

CHOICE Programme in the North Western Region

The CHOICE Programme was developed with older people in the Sligo, Leitrim and Donegal areas. CHOICE is underpinned by a philosophy of care based on the principles of respect, dignity and choice; it is person-centred, holistic and needs driven. It has been official policy in the North Western Region since February 2002. Based on the findings of surveys of older people undertaken in Sligo, Leitrim and Donegal, it responds to older people's preferences to live at home as they grow older, to remain independent and to avail of individualised and flexible services. Funding has been made available for the employment of an Active Age Officer and a Health Promotion Officer is employed to coordinate positive age awareness.

Source: CHOICE Programme, 2002, 2003

3.7 ● The quality of housing in Ireland has generally improved over the years. However, a recent survey of housing quality found that those aged 65 and over living alone were twice as likely as the average to report a major problem with their dwelling, for example in relation to dampness, food preparation facilities, sanitary facilities or ventilation (Watson and William, 2003 p.133). The periodic assessment of housing needs carried out by the local authorities also indicates that a significant number of older people experience housing difficulties. The 2002 assessment classified 3,215 older people as in need of housing and unable to provide it from their own resources, representing 6.6 per cent of the total housing needs identified (Department of the Environment, Heritage and Local Government, 2002, p.59).

A number of schemes have been put in place to improve the housing conditions of older people and these are outlined in Box 3.3 p.46. As can be seen from the list of schemes available to older people, there is considerable recognition of the importance of good quality housing to older people's independence. Key questions to be raised, however, are:

• the extent to which schemes dovetail with each other;

• consistency in terms of how the schemes are administrated at local level;

• the efficiency of having a number of schemes;

• their timeliness (in terms of the application process); and

• their impact on older people's quality of life.

The Team recommends that the Department of the Environment, Heritage and Local Government should develop and strengthen its on-going evaluation and assessment of the housing schemes, focusing in particular on efficiency and equity issues and older people's quality of life outcomes.

3.8 ● As part of the Team's consultations a number of general housing-related issues were raised and observations made, which are listed below:

- It is difficult for many older people to access the different housing grant schemes and the forms involved are not user-friendly. Co-ordination between schemes is poor. Better co-ordination between housing and health services is needed to develop more timely and person-centred service responses.

- The housing needs of vulnerable older people require specialised attention, for example, those with a disability, those released from institutions, the homeless.

- Technology could be better used to reach out to isolated older people in their own homes (eg social alarms and telephone monitoring).

- Older people's expectations and preferences in relation to housing are changing over time and these should be monitored and responded to.

- Due to house price increases, on leaving home, young adults can find it difficult to afford accommodation near their parents and this may have long-term implications for informal care.

- The development of universal design (designing homes and environments that are usable by most people regardless of their level of ability or disability) should be encouraged. Part M of the Housing Regulations, which specifies that adequate provision be made when building to enable people with disabilities to safely and independently access and use a building (Department of the Environment, Heritage and Local Government, 2004), is a positive step in this regard. But more generally, there is a need to consider how planning and design can support older people in the community.

- Ongoing home maintenance (gardening, painting, cleaning drains, etc) may be a significant worry for some older people, and help with general 'low level' home supports (see Box 3.5 p.50) could be very efficient in supporting older people to stay in their own homes for longer.

- Concern was expressed about the difficulties some older people experience in heating their homes, often due to a combination of low income, poor housing conditions and the lack of proper insulation.

- In relation to the local authority differential rent scheme, increases in pensions should not be automatically eroded by resultant increases in rent.

- Moving house may be the most appropriate way for some older people to meet their changing housing requirements. Ideally, this move should be within the locality and close to local services. Possible barriers to moving include the lack of a suitable housing-mix within communities, an issue which requires the attention of planners, and Stamp Duty disincentives for older owner-occupiers.

Box 3.3

Schemes Addressing the Housing Needs of Older People

Scheme	Details
■ Special Housing Aid for the Elderly Scheme	■ Operating since 1982, this Scheme is administrated by a central Task Force and operated by the Community Care sections of the HSE. Typically aid is available for necessary repairs to make a dwelling habitable for the lifetime of the occupant, including roofing, electrics, heating, repair or replacement of doors, guttering and windows, damp proofing. 22, 419 households have been assisted under the Scheme at a cost of €60 million over the period 2000 to 2004. The 2005 budget for the Scheme is €16.6 million.
■ Essential Repairs Grant Scheme	■ This Scheme is directed primarily at older persons living in poor housing conditions and is a 100 per cent grant of up to €9,523 towards repairs to prolong the useful life of a dwelling. 11,500 grants were paid over the period 2000 to 2004 at a cost of €53 million.
■ Disabled Persons Grant Scheme	■ This is a 90 per cent grant of up to €20,320 towards the adaptation of an existing house to meet the needs of a disabled person. 25,500 grants have been paid over the period 2000 to 2004 at a cost of €217.5 million. The scheme is currently under review.
■ Capital Assistance Scheme	■ This Scheme assists approved voluntary housing bodies to provide accommodation to meet special housing needs, for example sheltered housing for older people. In the period 2000 – 2004, €408 million has been provided and 3,942 units of accommodation built, of which 40 per cent were targeted at older people. The 2005 budget was €102 million.
■ Central Heating Programme for Local Authority Dwellings	■ Introduced in July 2004, the objective of this initiative is to assist local authorities in providing central heating facilities in their rental dwellings which lack them. The budget for the programme was €30 million in 2005.
■ Communal Facilities Grant	■ A grant scheme, up to €5,800 per unit, to housing associations to build a communal building or room to provide for additional activities that are carried out by the association. A total of €2.1 million has been allocated under the scheme for 2005.
■ Community Support for Older People	■ Operated by the Department of Community, Rural and Gaeltacht Affairs through voluntary or community-based groups to improve the security of older people in their area, including the installation of locks, security lighting, smoke and alarm systems.

Source: Data supplied by the Department of the Environment, Heritage and Local Government.

3.9 ● The Team recommends that the Department of the Environment, Heritage and Local Government should undertake research to assess older people's housing preferences and identify and address potential barriers or disincentives to their moving to the accommodation which best fits their needs.

3.10 ● The voluntary housing sector has to date provided in the region of 7,000 housing units for vulnerable or low income older people, two-thirds of which are low support and the remainder in the form of sheltered housing. Most of this housing was provided under the Capital Assistance Scheme (see Box 3.3 above) and such accommodation was considered to have positive aspects both for older people, in the form of better quality of life, and also savings for the Exchequer, as it is much cheaper than nursing home care. Concern has been raised, however, regarding the fragmentation between the housing and health aspects of this type of accommodation (Irish Council for Social Housing, 2005). Local authorities have also played an important role in the direct provision of housing for older people; currently authorities have about 13,000 units specifically for this group.

3.11 ● The Team recommends that the role of assisted and supported housing should be expanded as a housing option for older people, particularly where it supports independent living and a continuum of care. This will require the development of a strategic framework for housing and care. In considering the future of the voluntary sector in particular, the following issues require consideration:

• **FUNDING** – the adequacy of capital funding to develop high quality schemes and the development of a current funding scheme to assist care and support services.

• **SERVICES AND SUPPORTS** – the potential role of the sector in providing higher-level supports to residents in sheltered housing schemes, to help delay or prevent nursing home admission, the development of service standards and the development of housing schemes as hubs for services to the wider community where appropriate.

• **PLANNING ISSUES** – access to appropriate sites and ways to address delays in the planning process.

• **CO-ORDINATION** – co-ordination at central Government level and at local level between health and local authority sectors to develop clear policies and responsibilities in relation to the provision of housing and care.

Transport

3.12 ● Access to transport was a second key theme highlighted in the Team's consultations and in the written submissions received, especially the availability of public transport in rural areas. Where public transport schemes were in operation, they were seen as a vital support to older people, in terms of accessing health and other services, maintaining social networks and remaining active. Where this was problematic, however, it was identified as a considerable barrier to community-based living. Box 3.4 below outlines details of the Rural Transport Initiative, which has proved successful in the development of community-based rural transport projects.

3.13 ● The Public Transport Partnership Forum (PTPF) was established in 2000 under the National Agreement *Programme for Prosperity and Fairness (2000 – 2002)* to provide a mechanism for consultation on public transport matters and the development of ideas for the improvement of the sector. A sub-group of the PTPF has been established to examine the transport needs of older people in rural areas. The Sub-Group will examine the availability of public transport for older people in rural areas, the impact of the Rural Transport Initiative, strategies which might meet the needs of older people in rural areas, such as the expansion of the Rural Transport Initiative and or the use of school or other specialised transport services, the introduction of a voucher scheme for taxi and hackney services for older people to access scheduled and other services.

Box 3.4

The Rural Transport Initiative

The Rural Transport Initiative (RTI) aims to promote and support the development of community-based public transport projects in rural areas. It was launched in 2001 as a pilot initiative under the National Development Plan 2000-2006. The Scheme is administered by Area Development Management Ltd (ADM) on behalf of the Department of Transport and involves 34 schemes in 25 counties.

The type of service provided varies from scheme to scheme, but most contract out either some or all of their services to commercial operators (29 groups). Just under one-third of groups own and operate their own buses, and a small number operate community car share schemes and broker services with other organisations. An estimated 500,000 passengers used the service in 2004, two-thirds (66 per cent) of whom were aged 66 years and over. Most journeys (82 per cent) were pre-booked and most (79 per cent) were door-to-door. An independent evaluation of the scheme undertaken by Fitzpatricks Associates (2004) found that the RTI Scheme was an innovative and targeted service, which improved users' quality of life, promoted their independence and health and benefited the wider community, local development groups and transport providers. The evaluation recommended that the pilot phase of the scheme be extended to 2006 and that there should be an effort to improve links with local authorities and public service providers.

In response to this evaluation, the Minister for Transport announced in April 2005, that the RTI pilot scheme will be extended to the end of 2006, with his Department providing an increase in funding for 2005 (€4.5 million) and 2006 (€5 million) and will be made permanent from 2007.

Developing Community-based Provision

3.14 ● The Team's support for the development of community-based provision is based on research findings that preventative and low-level supports can have better outcomes for older people compared to interventions which are only provided at crisis points. Research from England indicates that relatively modest services, if provided at the right time, can have a major impact on older people's quality of life and can reduce mortality and admissions to long-term care. Elkan *et al* (2001) reviewed fifteen studies of the effectiveness of home visiting programmes that offer health promotion and preventative care to older people and found that home visits can reduce mortality and admission to long term institutional care. The paper pointed out that, historically these visits were provided to mothers and young children rather than older people, but they could also play a role in health promotion and preventative care for older people.

3.15 ● Box 3.5 overleaf lists the types of preventative interventions which could improve quality of life for older people and help prevent or delay the need for long-term care. These cover the home and the external environment and also relate to physical and practical interventions and personal and social interventions. It illustrates a number of points. Firstly, an effective preventative approach on the ground needs to cover the broader aspects of people's day-to-day lives, not just housing, health and care. Secondly, service responses need to be timely, flexible and co-ordinated. Thirdly, consultation with older people (and their carers where possible) about what their requirements might be is central to effective service responses.

3.16 ● The value of providing home-based care is well recognised in the Irish situation, but to date has not been well developed. As indicated above in Section 1, the Partnership Agreement *Sustaining Progress,* made a commitment to consider the implementation of a pilot programme of care in respect of older people (Department of the Taoiseach, 2003, 2.6.3) and in 2004 €1.25m was allocated to the development of homecare packages and in 2005 this was increased to €2 million.

3.17 ● One of the pilot programmes to emerge from this funding is the Slán Abhaile Project which is based in the East Coast Area of the Health Service Executive. It is targeted at older people who, in spite of their wish to remain living in their own homes, might be at risk of having to move into residential care in order to have their long-terms needs met. The pilot project aims to provide older people with a practical alternative to long-stay residential care by providing enhanced home support services. It has been in operation since May 2003 and an evaluation of the first year and a half of the project undertaken by the Economics Department of NUI, Galway found that it is cost effective when the public expenditure costs are compared with the cost of nursing home and hospital care (Health Service Executive East Coast Area, 2005).

Box 3.5

Examples of Low Level Services Which Could Improve Quality of Life and Prevent or Delay Long-term Care

	Home	External Environment
Physical and Practical	▪ Heating/insulation ▪ Security ▪ Cleaning ▪ Shopping ▪ Gardening ▪ Equipment/Adaptations ▪ Use of technology ▪ Life-time Housing ▪ Equity release	▪ Transport ▪ Personal safety ▪ Street lighting ▪ Built environment (eg pavements, disability access) ▪ Community centres ▪ Advice centres and One-stop-shops ▪ Accessible shops and affordable products
Personal and Social	▪ Befriending ▪ Carer supports ▪ Bathing ▪ Meals service ▪ Hairdressing ▪ Rehabilitation ▪ Personal care, including nursing, home help ▪ Advocacy ▪ Sheltered housing ▪ Rapid response ▪ Intensive home support	▪ Leisure ▪ Primary care ▪ Chiropody ▪ Lifelong learning ▪ Libraries ▪ Employment ▪ Volunteering ▪ Day care ▪ Luncheon clubs ▪ Rehabilitation ▪ Step-up/down schemes ▪ Engagement in setting of priorities ▪ Community development ▪ Healthy living schemes ▪ Peer support

Source: adapted from Joseph Rowntree Foundation Task Group on Housing, Money and Care for Older People (2003).

3.18 ● During this first eighteen months of the project, sixty-two people received the services, the average age of recipients being over 82 years. The project tapped into existing services, but additional services included:

• enhanced home support services, in the form of out-of-hours services, home support workers trained to undertake both personal and domestic care and high levels of flexibility;

• care coordination and case management provided by full-time care coordinators to develop integrated individual service plans (i.e. a schedule of all of the services that an older person needs in order to continue living at home), to advocate on behalf of the older person, coordinate service and monitor and review the plans;

• additional Occupational Therapy (OT) posts to facilitate a fast-track OT service and a dedicated equipment budget was included.

3.19 ● The evaluation also identified a number of challenges that need to be considered, namely:

• **SERVICE CAPACITY** – even with additional funding, it was not always possible to increase service capacity to the extent required because of staff shortages, for example in home support services. The evaluation called for the development of a career structure for home support staff, the adjustment of salary scales and additional ways to support people who are employed in this capacity.

• **SCOPE OF SERVICE** – the project was not able to accept people who required overnight care or all day supervision (e.g. people with dementia who live alone) because of the required additional resources. The evaluation called for greater clarity regarding the extent to which the HSE should be responsible for high dependency care support at home.

• **EQUITY BETWEEN OLDER PEOPLE IN SIMILAR CIRCUMSTANCES** – access to the Slán Abhaile service meant fast track access to other services, such as Occupational Therapy, with no means-test. Others in similar circumstances but not part of the project, were means-tested and on waiting lists for services.

• **INTERAGENCY/INTERDISCIPLINARY COOPERATION AND UNDERSTANDING** – difficulties were experienced in developing services at the interface between hospital and community and between and across health care disciplines. The evaluation concluded that strong commitment from senior management and time to define roles and procedures and build mutual understanding between project partners was needed.

3.20 ● Homecare grant schemes were also introduced in the Northern Area Health Board (end 2001) and the East Coast Area Heath Board (July 2002) to fund additional home support to eliminate or delay the need for institutional care. An evaluation of the schemes endorsed their general philosophy and approach, but recommended the introduction of a uniform assessment tool and regular re-assessment, more careful monitoring of the quality and adequacy of services, assessment of ability to pay and adequacy of payment in relation to actual costs of care, budgetary clarity and adequate staffing, including care and case management (Timonen, 2004). In Section 5 of the report, the Team considers care and case management approaches to developing a more co-ordinated and planned response to older people's care needs.

Community-based Subventions

3.21 ● The policy of promoting care at home requires that the supports available for home living are on a par with those available for institutional living. This is not the case at present. For example:

- an older person may qualify for a private nursing home subvention but not be able to convert that into a care subvention to live at home;

- tax relief that is available to the person who pays the nursing home fees is not available for contracted nursing care at home. Relief is available for those who employ, directly or through an agency, a person to take care of an incapacitated individual at home. The person must be incapacitated on or before the start of the tax year through to the end of the tax year. About 500 people claim this relief each year (that equals about 0.3 per cent of unpaid carers, see 3.28 p.54) at a total cost of less than one million euro per annum (Office of the Revenue Commissioners, 2003, Table IT6). Comparable figures are not available on the numbers claiming tax relief on nursing home fees;

- there is no comprehensive assessment of need for community care services. The only assessment is in relation to admission to either a public long stay place or in connection with the nursing home subvention.

3.22 ● The development of community-based subventions should be considered in the context of the overall objectives underpinning the financing of care for older people. The following principles have been suggested:

- The funding of long-term care should be comprehensive.

- Funding should not determine care requirements; rather care requirements should determine funding.

- There should be a built-in bias towards homecare solutions while retaining a capacity for financing care in institutionalised settings.

- Payment mechanisms should be prospective ('up-front') and case management should be used to determine needs.

- Access should be on the basis of need and should not be impeded by an inability to pay.

- Efficiency and the quality of care should be enhanced rather than diminished by the financing system (O'Shea, *et al*, 1995).

3.23 ● Community-based subventions have a number of clear advantages:

- They support older people's preferences and the stated policy objective of supporting older people to live at home for as long as possible.

- The grants are cost-effective compared to the cost of nursing home or extended hospital care for all but the highest levels of dependency.

- They address carer stress and help avoid nursing home admissions.

- Older people and their families have a greater say regarding the source and types of care services engaged.

- An evaluation of pilot home grants schemes found high satisfaction levels among grant recipients.

- Evidence from other countries with home grant programmes suggests that they may stimulate employment creation in the area of care services for older people (Timonen, 2004).

3.24 ● The Team strongly supports the concept of community-based subventions to contribute towards the care needs of those in community settings, and argue that these should be:

- available in all areas;

- based on a standardised application process, including standardised assessment of need, financial means and availability of support from other sources;

- designed to encourage flexible, recipient-centred and timely service delivery;

- realistic in relation to the cost of care services;

- monitored to ensure quality;

- well and clearly advertised;

- clear in terms of entitlement;

- based on case management to co-ordinate assessments and services;

- user-centred, promoting user-involvement in planning and purchasing of services;

- funded from a dedicated budget;

- part of a package which supports informal care, where available;

- planned to involve regular case review; and

- outcome focused, incorporating data collection to measure service outcomes and recipient satisfaction levels.

3.25 ● **The Team recommends that community-based financial or other supports for services should be made more widespread, focusing initially on high-dependent older people in the community and drawing on best practice from the pilot programme of care for older people (under the**

National Agreement Sustaining Progress); and that consideration should be given on equity and efficiency grounds to re-balancing the financial supports to different people in different situations (e.g. community and residential settings).

Carer Supports

3.26 ● Informal carers are a key resource which support and underpin many older people's preference to live at home. In Report Number 23 *A Strategic Policy Framework for Equality Issues,* the NESF drew attention to the importance of the affective dimension of equality (in addition to the economic, social and political aspects). This refers to the emotional and intimate aspects of human life and to the shared experiences of dependency and interdependency. The NESF concluded that the objective of affective equality challenges us to, for example: develop a public focus on care, design supports to enrich caring and respond to the needs of carers and dependents (National Economic and Social Forum, 2002).

3.27 ● The Census of Population 2002 indicated that there were 148,754 people who provided regular, unpaid personal help for a friend or family member with a long-term illness, health problem or disability in Ireland, or about 5 per cent of the adult population. The Census also found that about six out of ten (61 per cent) carers were women; one in ten (11 per cent) were aged 65 years and over, most of whom are married (67 per cent) and half of whom provided 43 or more hours care per week.

3.28 ● Informal caring performs a number of important functions, namely:

• It is an expression of inter-generational solidarity. Over half of carers care for a parent or parent-in-law (cited in Cullen, *et al*, 2004).

• It is essential to the implementation of Government policy to maintain older people in dignity and independence in their own home and to encourage and support the care of older people in their own community.

• It affords considerable savings to the Exchequer. The 150,000 carers provide up to 3 million hours caring every week resulting in saving to the Exchequer of up to €2 billion each year (The Carers' Association, 2005).

Informal care also has cost implications for carers, most obviously in terms of lost earning opportunities and pension entitlements; but and also more indirectly, where the strain of caring has a negative impact on the carer's own health.[2]

3.29 ● The Oireachtas Joint Committee on Social and Family Affairs, as part of its work programme 2002/3, reviewed the position of full-time carers. The Committee supported the following three principles, which had earlier been delineated by O'Shea *et al* (1995, see 3.22 above):

---

[2] *See presentation by Mr Ilija Batljan (Special Advisor to the Swedish Ministry of Health and Social Affairs) on* Care for the Elderly as an Investment in the Future *to the NESF Plenary on Care for Older People in the Royal Hospital Kilmainham 28 September 2005 at www.nesf.ie*

- Funding should not determine care requirements; rather, care requirements should determine funding.

- There should be a built-in bias towards homecare solutions while retaining a capacity for financing care in institutional settings.

- Access should be on the basis of need and should not be impeded by an inability to pay or by geography.

The Committee made a number of recommendations, including: a significant shift of resources towards homecare, the establishment of a consistent and comprehensive system of needs assessment, more flexibility in relation to respite care, changes in welfare entitlements for carers, better information, the development of a national strategy for family carers and that health and social services work more closely with carers and care recipients.

3.30 ● In light of the Committee's work and additional work nearing completion in the Equality Authority on *Implementing Equality for Family Carers* and to avoid duplication and overlap, the Project Team agreed it would not focus in on this area. The Team strongly supports, however, the view that carers are a core element of any community care strategy to facilitate older people to live in their own communities for as long as possible. Insufficient policy attention has been given to this area in the past and what is required now is a national strategy for caring.

The Team recommends that the Departments of Health and Children and Social and Family Affairs should jointly establish a broad-based group (including relevant Social Partners, Carers' groups and experts) to develop a National Strategy for Carers. This should give particular attention to the specific needs of older carers and should be completed within 12 months.

Conclusion

3.31 ● While the majority of older people live independent lives, it is nonetheless important that services are in place to delay the onset of dependency and to support independence were possible. As this Section outlined, this involves an integrated approach to the planning and delivery of services. It also involves a mindset change to put the older person at the centre of service delivery. There is much innovation in this area, but the lessons from pilot projects need to be implemented more widely and mainstreamed.

3.32 ● A recurring issue in the Team's work has been the consequences of policies which have favoured the growth of institution-based over community-based responses to care needs. One reason put forward for this situation is an imbalance in legislative underpinnings between the two sectors. In the next Section of the report, the Team examines the legal dimension to community-based care in more detail.

IV

Legal Aspects of Community Care

Introduction

4.1 ● The lack of a legal base to community care services for older people has
been identified as a potential barrier to the development of the sector, and
subsequently as a reason why some older people are unable to stay living
in their own homes for longer. This Section of the report focuses on the
legal dimension to community care for older people in Ireland and
specifically addresses two issues[3]:

* whether there should be a rights-based approach to community care
services for older people and, if so, what the practical effect of that would
be; and

* the practical barriers to community groups developing locally-based
community care responses for older people.

Rights-based Approach

4.2 ● The rights-based approach to services has developed largely in the
context of rights for people with disabilities. It can also be applied to other
areas, for example anti-poverty strategies. There is no one single definition
of a rights-based approach, but it is based on the view that people's rights
to services should be clearly set out in legislation, that rights to services
should be consistent and fair and that those services should be delivered
in a timely basis and in a manner which is respectful of the rights and
dignity of all people. It is usually contrasted with the 'charity' or discretionary approach to services which is considered likely to be inequitable
and unfair and not to require the service providers to implement policy
decisions nor the Government to provide the required funding.

[3] The Project Team wish to acknowledge the assistance of Ita Mangan, B.L. in the preparation of this Section of the report.

4.3 ● Inherent in a rights-based approach is the question of empowerment of the relevant group to make their own choices, advocate for themselves and exercise control over their lives. If people have legal rights, then others have legal obligations. The service providers are obliged to respect, protect and fulfil the rights of the service recipients. This obligation applies to the service providers in their capacity as providers and also in their relationship to private sector providers – they must ensure that private sector providers also respect, protect and fulfil the rights of service recipients. The rights-based approach requires that, as well as substantive rights (for example, to a home help service), there must also be the procedural and ancillary rights such as the right to information, to an adequate remedy and to participate in decision-making.

The Anti rights-based view

4.4 ● International human rights instruments are mainly concerned with broad civil and political rights and opponents of the rights-based approach argue that these rights are, in effect, fundamental and overarching rights (sometimes called 'hard rights') which require protection but that this does not apply to the social and economic rights (soft rights). It can be argued that some of the international instruments recognise this distinction in that the civil and political right must be 'ensured' while the social and economic rights must be 'recognised' and/or 'progressively realised'.

4.5 ● On this basis, social and economic rights are seen as basic needs which should be met by appropriate policies. Governments should have the right to decide on the allocation of resources for the implementation of social and economic policies and elevating them to the status of rights is an inappropriate interference in the democratic decision-making process. Economic development requires the satisfaction of needs in an environment where individual human rights must give way to community welfare. Rights-based legislation is likely to result in resources being wasted in litigation. It is sometimes argued that a rights-based approach involves a change in the relationship between the Executive and Legislative branches of government on the one hand and the Judicial branch on the other with the result that decisions on allocation of resources are made by the Judiciary instead of the democratically elected legislature and Executive.

The Pro rights-based view

4.6 ● Proponents of the rights-based approach argue that social and economic rights are inextricably interconnected with civil and political rights. It is not possible to be an active citizen and enjoy civil and political rights without appropriate economic, social and cultural rights. The absence of clear rights to services means that:

• A person's need for services is seen as a problem for the person rather than a problem for society as a whole (this broadly underlies the distinction between the medical and social models of disability).

- A person may not get any services or may get them on a discretionary basis only; this inevitably leads to inequity and inequality in service provision.

- The person has no access to a remedy if there is inequity or inequality in the provision of the service.

- Service providers have no obligations to people who need services.

4.7 ● The rights-based approach means that the economically weaker groups in society can be protected by the Judiciary from the economically powerful who can influence the allocation of resources by the Executive. It can be argued that rights may not be enforced until there is litigation. There is no doubt that the enforcement of the rights of children with disabilities to education has happened on foot of litigation. The right existed in the Constitution of Ireland but it was not recognised or enforced until court cases were taken. The enforcement of rights by litigation however has disadvantages. The service provider may simply grant the right to the complainant but a general principle that can be applied more widely is not established.

4.8 ● Unlike the case of children and education, most social and economic rights do not derive from the Constitution but from statute law. Such rights, even if they are clear and unequivocal, are not always enforced. It must be pointed out that it is remarkable how infrequently older people have taken cases to court on the basis of existing statutory rights, for example, in relation to public long stay care and nursing home subventions and the discretion in relation to medical cards.

What would a rights-based approach mean for older people?

4.9 ● At present, people do have a right to some community care services while others are entirely discretionary. Nursing care and home help are probably the main components of community care. There is an essential difference in the legal arrangements for these two services. Under Sections 60-61 of the Health Act 1970 there is an *obligation* to provide nursing services while home helps *may* be provided. Section 60 of the Health Act 1970 provides for nursing services. As already highlighted in Section 1, this imbalance in legal entitlement is a barrier to the better development of community care services for older people.

4.10 ● The rights-based approach assumes that rights, once established, will actually be implemented. As is noted above, this is not always the case: for example, there is a clear legal right to a home nursing service but it is accepted that there are not enough nurses available and the range of services they provide is not adequate to maintain all older people at home.

Right to a remedy

4.11 ● A crucial aspect of the rights-based approach is that a remedy is available so that a person can ensure implementation, at least to some degree. Generally, it is only possible to pursue a remedy if there is a right. However, even if there is no clear right but adequate information is available about how a discretionary service is provided, it may be possible to pursue some remedy on the basis of being treated unequally. So, for example, a person could ask the Ombudsman to investigate the circumstances surrounding a refusal by the HSE to provide a home help service. The Ombudsman may be able to provide a remedy if it can be shown that the processes involved were not transparent or were inequitably applied. This still does not confer a right on the person to a service – it does, however, force the service provider to improve procedures and transparency.

4.12 ● At present, there is no independent complaints and appeals system for the health services, as there is for the social welfare and tax systems. The Health Act 2004 does provide for an independent complaints system but the relevant part of the Act has not been brought into effect. The right to an adequate remedy does not necessarily imply a right to pursue the remedy through the Courts. It may be pursued through specific enforcement mechanisms - for example, the Equality Tribunal or the Ombudsman.

4.13 ● It is not clear that the courts would get involved in the minutiae of rights implementation. For example, if there was a statutory right to a home help service, it is likely that the courts would state that the HSE was obliged to provide the service but would not get involved in the question of the extent of the service required.

Right to Information

4.14 ● Another important aspect of the rights-based approach is the right to information. This right already exists in Ireland under the Freedom of Information (FOI) legislation, which obliges public bodies to publish:

• the rules, procedures, practices, guidelines and interpretations used by them and the precedents kept by them for the purposes of decisions, determinations or recommendations in relation to schemes administered by them; and

• information about the way such schemes are administered.

4.15 ● However, it is a matter of serious concern to note that neither the Department of Health and Children nor the HSE have published details of how people qualify for services such as home helps. They give general information but do not publish information about the criterion or criteria used for establishing service prioritisation. This means that it is not possible to know whether or not an individual was treated correctly and, among other things, reduces the possibility of seeking a remedy.

Resources follow rights

4.16 ● It is generally argued that a clear legal entitlement to services would mean that resources would have to be allocated. There is not an absolute guarantee, however, that resources would follow the establishment of rights but it is likely that some additional resources would be made available. The establishment of rights inevitably results in greater public awareness and, therefore, greater demands for improved services.

Assessments of need for community care

4.17 ● All schemes and services have conditions attached. Unlike civil and political rights which generally apply to all adults, social and economic rights are generally applicable to some groups only. For example, there cannot be a universal right to a home nursing or home help service but there can be a right for those who need those services. The preliminary right must be the right to an assessment of need. The assessment of need would have to take into account the community and social needs as well as the medical needs of the person. There could then be a right to the necessary services. There are problems, of course, in any assessment process and the result may involve decisions about appropriate services which do not take account of the wishes of the older person concerned.

4.18 ● The establishment of a right to an assessment of need does not necessarily mean that the services will then be provided. Countries which have rights to assessment of need, for example, the UK, New Zealand and Australia, do not have a parallel right to the services. This also applies in the Disability Act, 2005.

4.19 ● The absence generally of a right to assessment of need is a significant gap in the Irish system. However the Disability Act, 2005 provides for the assessment of need for people with disabilities.[4] Some older people are likely to come under the definition of disability but many who need community care services will not. In particular, older people who need mainly social care will not come under its terms. The Act includes a provision that it may be implemented at different times for different age groups. If this were to be implemented in such a way that older people were given low priority, this would be a further case of ageism and age discrimination (see Section 2).

4.20 ● Some assessment of need is carried out if an older person is looking for a place in a public long stay institution or is applying for a nursing home subvention. The assessment for public places is not provided for in legislation and the HSE has not published detailed guidelines on the application process (nor did the Health Boards) – this is another example of their poor implementation of the FOI legislation. The assessment for nursing homes subventions is provided for in legislation and involves an assessment of dependency – this is mainly concerned with ability to carry out the tasks of daily living.

---

[4] *Under the Disability Act, a person has a disability if there is a substantial restriction in his/her capacity to carry on a profession, business or occupation or to participate in social or cultural life because of an enduring physical, sensory, mental health or intellectual impairment. For the purposes of the assessment of need, a "substantial restriction" means a restriction which is permanent or likely to be permanent, results in a significant difficulty in communication, learning or mobility. This definition is regarded as being too narrow and is one of the major sources of criticisms of the Bill by groups representing people with disabilities.*

Charging for Services

4.21 ● It is notable that the rights-based approach does not require that the services be provided free of charge, although many proponents of the approach seem to assume that the services will be free. There is nothing in the international rights instruments to suggest that services must be free. One of the fundamental social/political rights is the right of access to the courts. It is not generally considered that everyone should be able to exercise this right free of charge. Free legal access is available to people who cannot afford to pay.

4.22 ● So, it is possible to have a rights-based approach to services while charging for them in accordance with ability to pay. This, of course, raises many questions about what constitutes ability to pay, whether or not assets as well as income should be taken into account and what legal obligations there should be on families to support dependent members.

4.23 ● There is considerable reluctance among many people to be required to use their assets to finance care in later life. There is no rights-based reason why they should not be required to do so unless it would result in the impoverishment of spouses or other dependents. Parents have responsibilities towards their minor children but they have no responsibilities towards their adult children nor do the adult children have any legal right to inherit their parents' estates.

4.24 ● The assessment of family income for the purposes of nursing home subventions has now ended. In practice, many families actually have to contribute to the costs of home nursing or nursing home care if the parents cannot afford it. The tax relief available for expenditure by family members on homecare is not nearly as extensive or clear as that available for expenditure on nursing home care, and as the Team recommended in Section 3 above, this should be addressed.

4.25 ● There has never been a comprehensive debate in Ireland about the role of families in supporting dependent members. This is true of dependent children as well as dependent adults. Parents are legally responsible for supporting their children. Child Benefit is regarded by many as a contribution by the State to the costs of rearing children but there has not been any debate about the appropriate level of the State's contribution. Recently, Child Benefit is seen by some as a contribution towards the cost of childcare, with parents having the option of using it to help pay for child care or caring for the children themselves. There is no legal obligation on people to support older parents or other relatives. Many people recognise a moral obligation to do so but it is arguable that older people themselves do not want to be dependent on their children for support.

4.26 ● There is no equivalent of Child Benefit in the case of dependent older people and some older people get no direct State assistance towards the cost of their care. In the UK, for example, those who become ill or disabled on or after their 65th birthday and need help with personal care can claim Attendance Allowance, which is a tax-free benefit paid weekly (Disability

Living Allowance is paid to those aged under 65 in need of similar forms of care). Under the National Agreement *Programme for Prosperity and Fairness* a Working Group was established to examine the feasibility of introducing a cost of disability payment and the National Disability Authority commissioned research to quantify the additional costs involved (indecon International Economic Consultants, 2004). It is clear from the research that people with disabilities experience additional costs of living, related to for instance, heating, transport and general day-to-day living that are not covered by State assistance. The introduction of a cost of disability payment would help to equalise the cost of living they experience. As noted in Section 2 above, many older people already receive age-related additional allowances, such as the Free Travel Pass, Fuel Allowances and the Medical Card, which undoubtedly help to address these additional costs for some; however they are not related to severity of need and may not be availed of by all in the same way. In Section 3 (above) the Team called for the more widespread introduction of community-based subventions.

Barriers to Community Groups Developing Local Responses

4.27 ● Community groups who want to develop local responses to the community care needs of older people face problems which have as much to do with lack of co-ordination between the various statutory authorities (mainly the local authorities and the HSE) and funding sources with very specific narrow remits as with legal issues. The enactment of the Health Act 2004 may lead to improvements in the co-ordination of activities between health authorities and housing authorities.

Community Housing/Sheltered Housing

4.28 ● If a community group wants to, for instance, build sheltered housing or equivalent accommodation, there may be an issue as to whether this is to be regarded as housing, community care or institutional care. In order to get funds to build housing or sheltered accommodation, the group could form a voluntary housing organisation, get recognition from the Department of the Environment, Heritage and Local Government and then get the voluntary housing grants under the Capital Funding Schemes for the Provision of Rental Accommodation by Approved Housing Bodies (Voluntary & Co-Operative Housing) (see Section 3 above). Groups may be able to avail of other assistance such as community employment and social economy schemes but it is difficult at present to get workers for these schemes. Once the houses are built, there may be major problems in getting funding for providing support staff.

4.29 ● The legal basis for the scheme of grants to voluntary housing bodies is contained in Section 6 of the Housing (Miscellaneous Provisions) Act 1992 and the regulations[5] made under that Section. The Act provides that housing authorities may provide assistance to approved housing bodies on such terms and conditions as are determined by the authority.

4.30 ● The Department's memorandum[6] on the scheme states that it is not intended for the provision of residential care or nursing home accommodation where residents would require extensive medical, nursing or institutional type care. This seems to be an administrative policy decision by the Department – the legislation does not preclude the provision of such accommodation. The memorandum recognises circumstances where there should be co-operation between housing authorities and health authorities. It states:

"Health Boards provide a range of community care services and support and may contribute towards the running costs of providing support services in housing projects. Approved housing bodies should consult at an early stage with the appropriate health board in relation to proposals for the provision of sheltered housing, group homes or hostels for persons such as the elderly, persons with disabilities or handicapped or homeless persons who may need this type of supportive accommodation with various levels of on-site and/or visiting support services. Where such a project is proposed, the approved housing body should have adequate arrangements available for the operation of the type of support services envisaged."

4.31 ● The scheme does specifically provide for caretaker/welfare accommodation and makes particular provision for people with disabilities:

"some housing projects for persons with mental disabilities or handicaps require a higher ratio of carers to residents than a single caretaker unit of accommodation. These projects may proceed on the basis of shared funding assistance to the approved housing body between the housing authority and the relevant health board for the area in which the project is located".

4.32 ● There is no legal reason, therefore, why the housing authority could not make a funding arrangement with the health authorities for the provision of services for older people. If the services being provided bring the accommodation within the terms of the Nursing Home Act 1990 then it must be registered as a nursing home and meet the standards set out in the legislation. The definition of a nursing home under the Health (Nursing Homes) Act 1990 is "an institution for the care and maintenance of more than two dependent persons". There are some exclusions. Homes for 'mentally handicapped persons' are generally excluded from the nursing homes legislation which may explain why the housing authorities treat

---

[5] The relevant regulations are Housing (Accommodation Provided by Approved Bodies) Regulations 1992 (Statutory Instrument 86/1992) and the Housing (Accommodation Provided by Approved Bodies) Regulations 1992 (Amendment) 2002 (SI 106/2002).

[6] The Department of the Environment, Heritage and Local Government memorandum (2002) on the scheme is at: www.environ.ie

them differently from accommodation for older people. However, it is difficult to see why the requirement to register as a nursing home should be a barrier to getting housing authority funding – there does not appear to be any legal reason for this.

Role of health authorities

4.33 ● There is a general legal principle that bodies such as local authorities and health boards must have specific legal authority to engage in any activities – they do not have inherent powers to do things. The powers available to health boards to make arrangements with other bodies for the provision of services were somewhat confused but they did not prevent such arrangements. The Health Act 2004 may mean that there is now a clearer legal framework for co-operation by the Health Services Executive with other bodies such as local authorities and with voluntary and community bodies. However, some of the provisions of the Act are not entirely clear and it will be some time before the HSE interpretation of them becomes known.

Health Act 2004

4.34 ● The Health Act 2004[7] requires the HSE to, among other things, integrate the delivery of health and personal social services. It is also required to draw up a code of governance which will include a description of the methods to be used to bring about the integration of health and personal social services. The Minister for Health and Children said that this requirement was included in order to:

"address the criticism which has frequently been levelled at the health services that patients can get lost in the system when moving from one sector to another because of the lack of integration between the various settings."[8]

4.35 ● This requirement will not, in itself, improve integration between the health and housing services because housing is not a personal social service but it could lead to improvements in community care services for people who are leaving hospital.

Agreement with other public authorities

4.36 ● The HSE is also being required to have regard to the need to co-operate and co-ordinate its activities with those of other public authorities if the performance of their functions could affect the health of the public. Section 8 allows the HSE to enter into formal agreements with other public authorities and Section 9 allows for informal arrangements. This provides a clear legal basis for agreements on such matters as housing for older people whether that housing is meant to support independent living or to provide accommodation for dependent people.

---

[7] *Most of the Health Act 2004 came into effect on 1 January 2005. The parts which are not in effect deal mainly with the proposed new complaints system mentioned above and are not relevant to this Section of the report.*

[8] *Second Stage speech, Dáil Debates, 23 November 2004.*

Arrangements with voluntary and community groups

4.37 ● In performing its functions, the HSE must have regard to, among other things, services provided by voluntary and other bodies that are similar or ancillary to the services it is authorised to provide.

4.38 ● Section 38 of the Health Act provides for the HSE to make an arrangement with a person for the provision of a health or personal social service. It is not clear if this is meant to allow for arrangements with bodies (as distinct from individuals). It would seem to mean individual service providers only as Section 39 (see below) provides for both bodies and persons. If this is the case, there is nothing in the Act to replace the provisions whereby the Eastern Regional Health Authority had the right to make between three and five year contracts with voluntary bodies for the provision of services.

4.39 ● The main mechanism by which health boards supported voluntary groups in providing services for older people was 'Section 65'- grants. Section 65 of the Health Act 1953 has now been replaced by Section 39 of the Health Act 2004. This provides that the HSE may give assistance to any person or body that provides or proposes to provide a service similar or ancillary to a service that the HSE may provide. This allows for the making of grants to community and voluntary groups for the provision of health and personal social services.

4.40 ● The new Section 39 is broadly similar to Section 65 except that it allows for assistance to be given to a person as well as a body and the person need not be a service provider. This gives the HSE power to give direct financial help to a person who is, for example, caring for a person who needs nursing or hospital care.

Conclusion

4.41 ● The Team recommends that the Department of Health and Children should clarify older people's entitlement to community care services, for example, core services such as the home help service, meals-on-wheels, day care, respite care, therapeutic/paramedic services and assisted and supported housing within the next six months. The Department should also commit to the expansion of these core services to become more comprehensive. In keeping with the recently enacted Disability Act, 2005, the Team also recommends that older people should have a right to a holistic assessment of their needs.

V

Co-ordinated Approaches

Introduction

5.1 ● The need for more co-ordinated and integrated approaches to the planning and delivery of all public services has long been advocated. Some progress has been made in trying to improve services for older people. It is generally accepted, however, that a lot more could be done to improve their overall effectiveness. In this Section of the report, we examine the barriers to better co-ordination, from national to local level, and recommend a number of improvements to the current situation.

Barriers to Better Co-ordination

5.2 ● There are two main reasons why the need for more co-ordinated approaches have been stressed - firstly, this leads to better outcomes for older people and secondly it is more cost-effective and helps avoid duplication and waste. Better co-ordination of services, therefore, is not an end in itself, but a means to achieving better service outcomes for all, especially those with more complex or multiple needs, and better value for money.

5.3 ● The Working Party on Services for the Elderly, *The Years Ahead* (1988), identified the lack of co-ordination as a key concern to be addressed in the development of a more integrated care delivery system, as evidenced by:

• lack of co-ordination between and within statutory service providers;

• lack of co-ordination on hospital discharges;

• inadequate support for people caring for older people at home;

• separation of responsibility for community care, acute hospital, psychiatric and long-term care into two or three administrative programmes;

• lack of co-ordination between private nursing homes and health board services; and

• inadequate working relationship between relevant voluntary bodies and health boards. (Working Party on Services for Older People, 1988 p.40)

5.4 ● The Working Party recommended a model of co-ordination at national, regional, community care area and district levels to achieve better co-operation between different agencies within the health boards; different agencies within the public sector; and the public and voluntary sectors. An evaluation of the implementation of the Working Party's recommend-ations concluded that this model of co-ordination was implemented in a patchy way, with some areas developing a district approach and others not (Ruddle, 1998, p.69-90).

5.5 ● The National Council on Ageing and Older People, based on an evaluation of pilot projects on the co-ordination of services for older people at the local level, argued that a lack of a 'co-ordination ethos' was a real barrier to progress in this area and called for greater co-ordination at Departmental level, which would then permeate down to local level. This identified the following factors to achieve effective co-ordination:

• an ethos of co-ordination from national to local level;

• a shared understanding of what is involved and its value;

• organisational arrangements to underpin it;

• adequate resources to promote this approach;

• joint planning to aid joint working;

• partnership involving all relevant stakeholders;

• inter-disciplinary team approach; and

• key worker to facilitate co-ordination (National Council for the Elderly, 1992, p.171).

5.6 ● The development of more co-ordinated approaches to service planning and delivery is a complex issue and one which requires commitment, time and resources to implement. From the Team's consultations, it is clear that we are still some way off achieving the environment which would encourage and facilitate better co-ordination. At a national level, efforts to co-ordinate in a more formal way have proved difficult to sustain. At a local level, while key workers have been appointed to develop co-ordination, much remains to be done to bring planning and administrative systems closer together to improve service delivery. The Team now examines in more detail the issue of the co-ordination of policy development and then the issue of service delivery.

Co-ordinated Policy Development

5.7 ● Co-ordination has been an important feature of the Strategic Management Initiative (SMI), the framework for the public service modernisation process. It emphasised the importance of quality customer services, one of the principles of which was better coordination and a more integrated approach to service delivery. The SMI also stressed the need to develop new approaches at a cross-Departmental level to deal with pressing and complex issues, pointing out that in the Civil Service structure that existed in the mid 1990s "there are limited structures for consultation, co-ordination and co-operation and the current system rewards 'territorial protection' at the expense of active co-operation to achieve results." (Co-ordinating Group of Secretaries, 1996 p.15). An independent evaluation of the SMI concluded that it has had a positive impact on the overall effectiveness of the civil service, but identified cross-departmental collaboration and cross-divisional dialogue as areas in need of further attention (PA Consulting, 2002).

5.8 ● The review of the implementation of *The Years Ahead* report concluded that, while some collaboration was evident at national level, procedures remained, on the whole, informal and unstructured (Ruddle, *et al*, 1997 p.89). The need for and value of better co-ordination on matters relating to older people at a national level has been formally recognised with the establishment of the Inter-Departmental Group on the Needs of Older People. This Group was established in July 2002 and includes membership from a number of key Departments, with the following terms of reference:

- to examine, on an inter-Departmental basis, matters which impact on the lives of older people and to ensure that a co-ordinated approach is adopted in relation to them;

- to examine on a priority basis areas of particular difficulty and ensure that appropriate action is taken to resolve these;

- to follow up individual matters referred to it from time to time by the Minister of State; and

- to issue regular progress reports of its work.

5.9 ● The Group adopted a cross-cutting approach to its work, which focused initially on what was being done at present, with a view to bringing better co-ordination and integration between Departments and the various agencies. The Group engaged in a series of consultations with agencies and groups with responsibility for the delivery of services to older people, advisory agencies and groups and representatives of older people, culminating with a consultation conference (Inter-Departmental Group on the Needs of Older People, 2004). Issues warranting the particular attention of the Group included:

- housing matters and the various home improvement schemes;

- the information gathering process and the demands placed on older people by that process;

- the consolidation and simplification of applications forms;

- the security of older people; and

- equality matters in relation to older people.

5.10 ● While the work of this Group is valuable in the development of more co-ordinated approaches to planning and service delivery, the Team is concerned that the Inter-Departmental Group has been less active in recent months and that the momentum built up following its establishment may now be in danger of waning.

5.11 ● In the circumstances, the Team recommends that the Inter-Departmental Group on the Needs of Older People should be widened and strengthened to take on a stronger cross-Departmental remit with representatives at Assistant Secretary level and supported by a permanent and senior level Secretariat. This Group should:

• develop a National Strategy on Ageing (see 1.28 above);

• consider the structures, legislation and funding requirements and allocation needed to underpin cross-Departmental co-ordination and integrated planning; and

• support innovative approaches to local-level service co-ordination and disseminate good practice.

Co-ordinated Service Planning and Delivery

5.12 ● The co-ordination of service planning and delivery is perhaps the area that can have the most direct and immediate impact on older people's experiences as service users and also on service outcomes. A pre-condition for this is to have a full range of services available and accessible - for instance, health and social services, housing, transport, education and leisure. Throughout this report, the Team has stressed the need for a shift in mind-set from a 'one-size-fits-all' to one where the older person is at the centre of service delivery. The Team has argued that older people should not be stereotyped as dependent, frail, with little to contribute and needing intensive services. Instead, greater recognition of inter-generational interdependence and the importance of well-being in old age should be highlighted. It is important, therefore, that services are better co-ordinated and that older people are actively included in service planning and delivery.

5.13 ● The Team recommends that:

• Older people should have an active role in planning and service delivery at local level on an on-going basis, through consultation and participation.

• Issues of specific concern to older people should be addressed by local and regional planning fora, for example, the HSE Advisory Panels, the Strategic Planning Committees, Vocational Education Committees and the County and City Development Boards and older people should be specifically represented on these fora.

- Greater emphasis should be given to the role of co-ordinating staff in service planning and delivery and all service delivery staff should receive training in integrated service responses, standards should be set and best practice disseminated.

- Data gathering systems should be developed which are person-centred and have the capacity to be collated and analysed to plan appropriate responses for groups of older people (e.g. at community level or additional needs level).

- IT solutions should be developed to promote co-ordination and integration and also to promote assistive technology for independent living.

- The development of innovative approaches to service co-ordination (such as joint planning and budget sharing) should be supported and lessons learnt, disseminated and mainstreamed.

Integration at the Individual Level

5.14 ● Section 7.4(a) of the Health Act, 2004 requires the newly established Health Service Executive to integrate the delivery of health and personal social services, and the Team welcomes this provision. Integration of services at the individual level is the ultimate goal to be achieved, but this is only possible and sustainable in the context of a more co-ordinated approach to the planning and delivery of service at other levels.

5.15 ● Care and case management is an approach to more integrated care planning and delivery, particularly for older people with complex care needs. While there is some debate relating to the exact definition of care and case management, in general terms care management is the process of service co-ordination and planning at management level and case management is defined as the development of individually tailored care plans, with a person-centred and multi-disciplinary focus delivered through a case manager or team (Delaney, 2001 p.35). Seven core aims and principles of care management have been identified:

- empowerment of recipient of care and their informal carers to make informed choices about their care;

- a person-centred approach to care;

- integration and co-ordination of health and social services;

- increasing independence for care recipients;

- continuity of care – providing a seamless service;

- a holistic approach to care; and

- reducing the high costs associated with unnecessary admissions to institutional care (Delaney, 2001, p.62).

5.16 ● *The Health Strategy Primary Care: A New Direction* (2001) proposed the
introduction of an inter-disciplinary team-based approach to primary care
provision, with primary care teams to include, for example: GPs, nurses/
midwives, health care assistants, home helps, physiotherapists, occupational
therapists, social workers and administrative personnel. It is envisaged that
the primary care team will liaise with specialist teams in the community to
improve integration of care. The aims of this new approach are to
strengthen the primary care system so that it can play a more central role
as the first and ongoing point of contact for people with the health-care
system, provide a more integrated and co-ordinated service to the public
and enhance the system's capacity in areas such as personal social
services, rehabilitation and disease prevention. The Strategy proposed that
40-60 primary care teams will be in place by end 2006, with 400-600 in
place by end 2011. As detailed in Section 1 above, however, to-date only ten
initial teams have been established.

5.17 ● The international experience of care management for highly vulnerable
older people is that it can reduce institutional care placements, improve
quality of care and quality of life for older people and for their carers at
similar and sometimes lower cost, although in relation to dementia care
the cost was higher (Challis, 2002). There are barriers to its implementation,
however, which must be addressed, namely:

• it requires an anti-ageism service ethos (See Section 2 above);

• the older person's preferences must be at the centre of the approach;

• it is targeted at those most vulnerable;

• case managers require specific training;

• it depends on good inter-disciplinary teamwork; and

• to offer real choice to older people, case managers need to be able to offer
a range of services, which in turn requires them to have direct access to
resources and budgets (Delany, 2001).

5.18 ● The Team supports the development of this type of service planning,
which is multi-disciplinary, collaborative, co-ordinated, monitored and
evaluated, needs-lead and outcome driven.

The Team recommends that the Department of Health and Children and the
HSE should ensure that care and case management principles, philosophy
and approaches are embedded across the community care system and at the
point of admission to and discharge from residential and acute care services.

5.19 ● On a related point, the Team recommends that a unified and holistic
assessment process of establishing older people's needs for services should
be introduced as a priority. This does not mean that needs would be only
assessed once or by only one person, but that the collection of information
concerning a person's situation would be:

• **Timely** – as the assessment may be carried out at a potential crisis point,
such as hospital discharge or following a particular event.

- **POOLED** – at least basic information should be shared by different relevant professionals (to avoid duplication) and data should be collated for service planning purposes.

- **COMPREHENSIVE** – to include health, social care, housing and other needs.

- **RESOURCED** – so that information gathered can be responded to appropriately, with priority given to home-based solutions where possible.

- **MULTI-LAYERED** – from a basic assessment for straight-forward cases to the involvement of different specialists in more complex ones.

- **INFORMATIVE** of the range of services (statutory, voluntary and private) available to extend choice to older people.

- **PARTNERSHIP-BASED** and include the perspective of older people and, where appropriate, their carers and advocates.

- **OUTCOME FOCUSED,** with review timetables built-in where needed.

- **OF AN AGREED PROFESSIONAL STANDARD.**

In the context of older people's average low incomes (see Section 1), it is also important that the process includes an assessment of their ability to afford or pay for services.

5.20   In the development of models to implement such an assessment process, innovation is required to tackle some of the potential barriers. For instance, if information sharing is considered to be a potential problem, older people themselves should hold a master copy of their needs assessment, similar to a portfolio, which can be consulted and added to by different service providers over time as appropriate. If the disconnection of different administrative systems is found to be a barrier, planning networks need to be established and supported and consideration should be given to incentives for joint working, such as shared budgets, compatible IT systems and/or dedicated co-ordination staff. Implementation will also rely on the development of a clear vision of what is to be achieved, leadership to drive forward change and training to support new ways of working.

5.21   Box 5.1 below outlines the example of how an innovative rural area in the Netherlands recast its services to address rural decline. The success of this initiative resulted in positive outcomes for older people and the wider community, as well as Exchequer savings.

Box 5.1

Personalised Services for Older People in Trynwalden, the Netherlands

Trynwalden is a rural area in the Netherlands with a population of about 9,000 spread across seven villages. Since the mid 1990s it has developed a new approach to integrating housing, welfare, social services and care for older people. The initiative was developed as part of an effort to reverse rural decline in the area and involved the coming together of services providers (including budget pooling) and older people themselves. It attracted additional funding from a government modernisation of long-term care programme.

Personalised service brokers or 'Omtinker' are a key aspect of the initiative. They work like advocates for services users. Trynwalden has four teams of Omtinkers and they work outside the existing bureaucracies to organise the most suitable service for the individual older person, using vouchers within an internal market to buy the most appropriate services. They also ensure that users receive the services they requested and pass on complaints and grievances.

The initiative also has five multi-disciplinary teams who provide care support around the clock in the client's own home. Each team consists of home helps, home carers, nurses, social workers (and others on call, such as physiotherapists and GPs).

The care home in Trynwalden has been replaced with apartments equipped with the latest assistive technology and a central service centre provides a variety of social services for the whole community. The centre has an important remit in reinforcing and developing social networks and inter-generational links. A notable innovation is the 'care hotel', where people can stay after discharge from hospital and are cared for initially by a rehabilitation team and then the community-based multi-disciplinary team.

Residents of Trynwalden consume up to one-third less care compared to the Dutch national average, leading to government savings.

Source: www.skewiel-trynwalden.nl

Integrating Community and Residential Care

5.22 ● People's needs change over time and it is important that services co-ordinate with each other to ensure these are met in an efficient and effective way. Co-ordinating community and residential or institutional care is a key challenge in this regard. In this respect, shifting the emphasis of care to home or community-based solutions and preventing unnecessary admission to long-stay institutional care and delayed hospital discharges will involve:

• A CHANGE IN THE ROLE OF INSTITUTIONAL CARE – it needs to be widened and recast to take on a much more developed role in relation to respite, rehabilitation and re-integration (see also Section 7 p.91).

• A CHANGE IN THE DESIGN AND OPERATION OF INSTITUTIONAL CARE – greater emphasis should be put on reducing the 'institutional feel' of long-stay facilities: their design and layout should resemble community settings, with more emphasis given to the development of sheltered housing; and their day-to-day operation should avoid institutionalisation of residents and encourage independence.

- **THE DEVELOPMENT OF MORE INTERMEDIATE CARE, BETWEEN PRIMARY AND SPECIALIST SERVICES** – more step-up and step-down services are needed to help prevent unnecessary hospital admissions, support early discharge and reduce or delay the need for long-term residential care. These services could be provided at home, in community-based facilities or even more institutional setting but would usually be of short duration with a strong focus on rehabilitation and recovery and exploring alternatives to admission to long-stay care.

- **CONTINUITY AT COMMUNITY LEVEL** – community-based care services should be more linked-in to hospital and institutional settings, for example: regarding hospital or institutional care discharge needs assessments and the continuity of community contact when an older person is admitted to hospital (particularly where family or informal community links are not available).

In Section 7 of the Report, the Team focuses on the related topic of quality of care.

Conclusion

5.23 ● In this Section of the report the Team has stressed the importance of a more co-ordinated approach to service planning and delivery and has recommended that this should be activated from national to local level. This is not for co-ordination's sake alone, but should be clearly focused on improving the quality of service outcomes for older people and extending their choices. The Team summarises the overall proposed shift in approach in Box 5.2 overleaf.

Box 5.2

A New Approach to Planning and Delivering Care for Older People

Traditional Approach

- Ageing has a low and fragmented policy profile and lacks contemporary strategic vision

- Age-limits are an important aspect of how services are planned and delivered

- Focus on crisis interventions and institutional responses

- Departments and Agencies working independently of each other

- Lack of user involvement and consultation

- Informal carer involvement and support not prioritised

- Lack of focus on care staff training, accreditation and career progression

- Lack of focus on impact of services on older people's quality of life

- Budgets not adequate to needs

- Lack of voluntary and private sectors' input to policy and service development

New Approach

- Strategic policy response to ageing based on an understanding of older people as active citizens

- Needs assessment replaces age-limits in planning and service delivery

- Focus on well-being, prolonging independence, rehabilitation and social engagement

- Co-ordinated planning and timely delivery of services from national to local levels

- Strong focus on user empowerment, involvement and consultation

- Informal carers actively involved and supported in their role

- Care staff ongoing development and training valued, planned and supported.

- Monitoring and evaluation of service outcomes

- Realistic budgeting directed to quality and effective services

- Voluntary and private sectors actively involved in policy and service development.

5.24 ● So far, the Team has emphasised that many older people live very independent and healthy lives, and that the stereotype of them as a highly dependent group should be challenged. It is equally the case, however, that some older people are particularly vulnerable. One of the objectives of the NESF in its work is to consider the situation of those most marginalised and excluded in our society, and it is to these groups of older people that the Team's attention now turns.

VI

The Most Vulnerable

Introduction

6.1 ● Throughout this report, the Team has emphasised two important facts which are repeated here by way of introduction: firstly, that older people are not a homogenous group, but are as diverse as any other age group in society; and secondly, that the majority of older people live independent and active lives. The NESF has a particular mandate to consider the position of those who are most marginalised in society and this Section considers issues relating to those older people who are most vulnerable. In some cases this arises from earlier life histories, in other cases it may be more age-related and for some it may be a combination of both life events and the ageing process.

Recognising Diversity in Old Age

6.2 ● Recognising diversity in old age is an important principle in informing policy and service delivery. People aged 65 years and over make up slightly more than one-in-ten of the population, but some are much older, with over two-fifths (44 per cent) aged 75 years and over. As in the general population, most are married (47 per cent), more than the average are widowed (33 per cent), some are single (18 per cent), separated or divorced (2 per cent).

6.3 ● Many older people rely substantially on their pensions - over four-fifths of income in households with one or more older persons resident derives from pensions. It is noteworthy that older people face relatively high levels of income poverty, but report less enforced deprivation than other groups in terms of their access to basic lifestyle goods. This may be due to their ability to build up resources over their lifetime, or due to lower expectations. In either case, if a lot of older people are cash poor, a considerable number are also asset rich – with over four-fifths owning their own home.

6.4 ● Most older people report that they are in general good health, have a large network of friends, family and neighbours and are not socially isolated. Recent research found that while some experience loneliness, particularly with increasing age, lack of family and poorer health and social isolation, its prevalence is low (Treacy, *et al*, 2004). This is not to downplay the significant health and social problems experienced by some older people, which are discussed below.

Identifying Groups at Particular Risk

6.5 ● The development of policy and the delivery of services and supports for older people must balance the experiences of the majority of older people living an active and satisfying life with the specific needs of particular groups of older people whose needs may be different or more complex.

6.6 ● The Team identified the following groups of older people who may be considered to be at particular risk of marginalisation. In doing so, the Team recognised that individuals may move in and out of these situations over time and that vulnerability may not necessarily be cumulative. Some older people may also fit into more than one grouping at any one time, perhaps leading to multi-disadvantage. The Team also acknowledged that this list is in no way exhaustive, but rather illustrative of the heterogeneity of older people's situations. It is also further supports the need for person-centred service planning and delivery which has been a constant theme that we have made throughout this report.

- **The Homeless** – about 5 per cent of the homeless population are aged 65 and over and a further 40 per cent are aged between 40 and 64 (Williams and Gorby, 2002). Many of these may have physical and or mental ailments, which have developed at a younger age than the general population. As services improve it is likely that their life expectancy will too, and this will need to be responded to with innovative services that can adapt to complex individual requirements. Moving people on from emergency accommodation to more settled environments is important in this regard.

- **Members of the Traveller Community** – low life expectancy means that few Travellers live into old age. Older Travellers (i.e. those aged 65 years and over) account for just 3.3 per cent of the total Traveller population, compared with 11.1 per cent for the general population. Within the Traveller culture there is a tradition of family support for older people. This is a strength that should be built on and supported. It is important that services are culturally appropriate and that they are respectful of older Travellers' preferences, for example in relation to their accommodation choices.

- **Ethnic Minority Groups** – As Ireland becomes a more multi-cultural society it is important that services are delivered in a culturally and linguistically appropriate manner.

- **Older Disabled** - Almost one-third (31 per cent) of those aged 65 and over have a disability and 42 per cent of people with disabilities are in this age category (Central Statistics Office, 2004). About two-thirds of disabled people aged over 65 experience more than one kind of disability or restriction, with the incidence of multiple restrictions rising with age. Given this high overlap between disability and age it is important that services and funding mechanisms for those two groups are dovetailed appropriately.

— All those aged 70 years and over now receive a medical card and thus are eligible for assistive devices, however those under 70 years without a medical card have no entitlement to disability aids such as walking devices, hoists or other aids which could prolong independence.

— During the Team's consultations, the point was raised that the medical and physiological effects of ageing are often more pronounced in people with learning disabilities. For example, it was estimated that those with Down's Syndrome are 20 – 50 per cent more likely to develop Alzheimer's Disease than the general population and may develop it at an earlier age.

— The need for additional supports for adults with a disability living with their parents may also increase as they age. Similarly, the parents of those in residential settings may need additional supports over time to continue to visit and have an active part in their child's life.

— As discussed in Section 3 above, the built environment should be designed to accommodate the highest degree of access as possible for all.

The position of those with Dementia is discussed in more detail below.

• **ELDER ABUSE** – Studies indicate that in the region of 3 – 5 per cent of older people living in the community suffer abuse at any one time – that is in the region of 12,000 – 20,000 people. This estimate does not include those in institutional settings. A Working Group on Elder Abuse was established by the Minister of State at the Department of Health and Children in 1999 to examine this issue and it concluded that the response to elder abuse should be placed in the wider context of health and social care services for older people. The Group developed draft policies and procedures, which were piloted in two community care areas, following staff training. It made a number of recommendations, including:

— the formulation of a clear policy and staff structures to implement it at local level;

— greater legal protection and entitlement to core community care services,

— better supports for carers;

— a public awareness programme;

— staff training;

— specific protection against financial abuse; and

— access to an advocacy service for those in long-term residential care.

The Group also recommended that the Department of Health and Children should establish a National Implementation Group (established in June 2004) and fund a National Centre (Working Group on Elder Abuse, 2002). Funding of between €0.75m and €0.9m has been allocated each year between 2003 and 2005 to continue with the implementation of the report's recommendation. HSE Areas have undertaken various actions, including:

— the development of steering committees in HSE areas;

— the development of guidelines for the protection of vulnerable adults;

— training and education programmes for staff;

— the development of investigation procedures;

— information leaflets;

— the development of local standards for residential care for older people;

— appointing relevant staff;

— conducting research projects; and

— establishing a consumer panel for older people.

• **'Eccentrics' in the community** – this is a generic term used to describe a relatively small number of older people living in the community who engage in behaviour which is not considered the norm by society generally and may be unsafe for themselves or others. This might involve excessive hoarding or anti-social behaviour. It is important that an individual's right to be different is respected, but this also needs to be balanced with other people's entitlement to live in a safe and hygienic community and not to feel harassed. Specialised staff are needed in the development and delivery of services for this group, together with partnerships between local authorities and health services.

• **Lesbian, gay and bi-sexual older people** – in the NESF's previous work in this area, the issue of partnership rights for same-sex couples was raised, for example rights to nominate a partner or successor, to nominate a beneficiary of pensions and inheritance and to designate a next-of-kin for medical reasons. These may be particularly important for older lesbian, gay or bi-sexual people (National Economic and Social Forum, 2003).

• **Isolation** – those who are socially isolated are at increased risk of marginalisation, although one may not necessarily lead to the other. The risk of isolation may be increased for the very old, those with few family ties, those living alone, those with poor health, diminished sight or hearing, those with few social networks or social outings and those lacking transport, educational qualifications or income. Adequate transport, income, a choice of activities to attend, the development of visiting and befriending schemes, home supports, sheltered housing and information are all ways to address social isolation, but they need to be informed by personal choices and preferences (Tracey, 2004). In the written submission received by the Team (see Annex 3) difficulties faced by older people in accessing the Community Support for Older People Grant, which aims to improve the security of older people, were highlighted and many expressed concern about its application process. In particular, it was considered inappropriate that older people must apply for this grant through a relevant community or voluntary group, instead of being able to make an application themselves.

The Summerhill Active Retirement Group, detailed below in Box 6.1, is a good example of the value of community-based responses to counter isolation.

• **OLDER PEOPLE LEAVING INSTITUTIONAL CARE** – those who have had experiences of different types of institutional life, for example due to a mental health problem, alcohol addiction, intermittent homelessness, or having spent time in prison, may be particularly vulnerable in terms of their skills to deal with everyday life such as home and financial management, cooking and keeping themselves warm and clean. They may also be reluctant to avail of the services and supports available in the community.

Box 6.1

Summerhill Active Retirement Group

Summerhill Active Retirement Group was established in 1988 to help cater for the recreational needs of older people in Summerhill, Co Meath. The Group operates on the basis of its members' needs and aspirations and aims to provide information and new ideas that will encourage older people to improve their own lives and make a positive difference to their communities. The Group is based in the Third Age Centre and operates a number of activities, including: information on entitlements, rights, education, a community laundry service, craft activities, weekly visits from residents of the local nursing home, a bus service, a choir, computer and internet courses. The promotion of older people's rights and giving them a voice in society are key objectives of the Group and it lobbies for facilities, rights, opportunities and social inclusion of the older people.

The Group also operates the Senior Help Line, which is a confidential help line and listening service for older people. It runs 7 days a week, with 11 centres around the country and involves over 300 older volunteers. An independent evaluation found that it made a valuable contribution to the health and well-being of both users and older volunteers, at a relatively low cost, and called for it to be extended to become a branded national service for older people (O'Shea, 2004).

The Group recently ran a number of health programmes, including sessions on fitness, health checks, healthy eating, first aid and mental health. An independent evaluation found that the programme had significant positive benefits for many of the participants, particularly the social aspects. Overall the evaluation found that this Group promoted the general well-being of the older people involved and could have the long-term benefit of alleviating the pressure on primary healthcare services.

• **THE VERY OLD** – A written submission received by the Team summed up the vulnerabilities which can be faced by older women:

"Old age can be a particular challenge for women, the stats show that we live longer but quality of life may be an issue. We are often the informal, unpaid family carers, yet as we become older ourselves and outlive our partners and siblings, who is left to care for us? Is this issue recognised and what responses does the system make? We do not want to be a burden, but our choices are often very limited, with residential care often the only option or the predominant option, mindsets need to change on all sides, we need to be more assertive and the 'system' needs to see Older People in a new empowered light."

Poverty research indicates that older women, particularly those in rural areas, are particularly vulnerable to experiencing poverty and deprivation (Layte, *et al*, 1999, Nolan *et al*, 2002). Many older women are still affected by the traditional low rates of female labour force participation which were the norm during their working lives, supported by the marriage bar (which was lifted in the 1970s), lack of childcare, unequal pay and tax arrangements during that period. Lack of insurable contribution in their own right has meant a higher reliance on Non-Contributory pensions or a reliance on their spouse's insurance contributions.

• **OLDER BEREAVED** – The death of a spouse or close family member or friend at any time of life can be traumatic, but this may be particularly so for those in old age. It can leave an older person vulnerable on a number of fronts, for example: in terms of emotional or romantic loneliness, social isolation and financial stability. Simple activities such as doing the shopping, socialising, attending church or collecting the pension may suddenly become more difficult for those who relied on a spouse or friend for transport. Likewise day-to-day activities such as cooking and home maintenance may become more burdensome for those not used to doing these things for themselves. In other cases, the death of a spouse or carer may present difficult and immediate questions about who will take on the role of main carer.

6.7 ● These examples of vulnerability detailed above indicate the diversity of older people's experiences, both throughout life and also in old age. But there may be some common features of those most at risk, for example, there is a likelihood that they may lack access to financial resources, which otherwise might help to alleviate some of their vulnerability or they may lack family or social networks for support. The person-centred approach which the Team advocates in this report, should be designed to be able to incorporate general needs, preferences and choices with more specific ones on an individual basis.

Dealing with Dementia

6.8 ● Particular attention is given to those with dementia as the Team considers this group to be particularly vulnerable to exclusion and isolation. Dementia refers to a group of diseases, of which Alzheimer's disease is the most common, characterised by progressive and, in the majority of cases, irreversible decline in the mental functioning of sufferers. There is no single cause of dementia, nor is there yet a cure for the vast majority of dementias. It is not caused by ageing, nor is it inevitably part of the ageing process, but it is age-related. Studies on its prevalence, which seek to estimate the number of people with dementia at a given point in time, show a sharp rise in the prevalence of dementia with age, with the highest rates in the very oldest age categories. Although dementia is far less common in age categories below 60 years, when the disease does occur in younger age categories it poses different types of challenges for family carers and the health services.

6.9 ● The application of EURODEM[9] prevalence rates to the most recent Census of Population data for Ireland suggests that there are 34,097 people with dementia in the country, made up of 20,222 females and 13,875 males. This is an increase of just over 3,000 from 1996, when there were 31,000 people with dementia made up of 18,000 females and 13,000 males (O'Shea, *et al,* 1999). The total number of people with dementia is projected to grow, with the numbers increasing in line with the ageing of the population, and is predicted reach over 50,000 by 2021.

6.10 ● The vast majority of people with dementia (75%) live at home in the community. However, the majority of people living at home have never been formally diagnosed with dementia and most of them would not be known to the health and social care services. While early diagnosis is critical for the development of an optimal care plan, the reality is that early diagnosis is the exception rather than the rule. There are no general screening programmes for the disease and health care professionals, including general practitioners, are not always trained in the symptoms. Even when these are obvious, there may well be a reluctance to label someone with dementia because of the negative attitudes and stigma sometimes associated with the disease within families and communities. There may well also be an erroneous attitude that as nothing can be done for the patient in terms of a cure, it may be best not to create false expectations on behalf of patients or future demands on existing community care resources, which are already scarce.

6.11 ● It is no wonder, therefore, in such circumstances that families bear most of the cost of care for people with dementia. The overall baseline cost estimate for dementia in Ireland was €315 million in 2,000, suggesting an annual average cost of care per person of just over €10,000 (O'Shea and O'Reilly, 1999). Community care accounts for less than one tenth of overall

---

[9] *EURODEM applies average dementia rates across the EU to our Census data to estimate prevalence rates.*

costs, mainly because of the weakness of community care generally, and the absence of specific services for people with dementia. Family care accounts for over 50% of the overall burden of care. There are an estimated 50,000 carers in Ireland looking after someone with one of six specified symptoms of dementia: for example 25,000 carers are looking after someone with marked forgetfulness on a regular or occasional basis, while 15,000 are looking after someone with confusion to the point of interfering with everyday life. Caring for people with dementia is a source of major strain and psychological distress for carers with the majority scoring poorly on the General Health Questionnaire and two thirds reporting that the job of caring is completely overwhelming at times (O'Shea, 2003).

6.12 ● Dementia is a relatively new area of policy focus compared to many other of the diseases and conditions which impose a large burden on society. Few countries have specific policies for the condition and where there is a policy it is mostly encompassed in wider generic policies and statements on ageing. In addition, discussions of policy issues are relatively rare in the research literature (OECD, 2004). In Ireland the stated objective of public policy for people with dementia is to encourage and facilitate their continued living in their own homes for as long as is possible and practicable (*The Years Ahead*, 1988).

6.13 ● *The Action Plan for Dementia* (National Council on Ageing and Older People, 1999) reinforced the need for a social model of dementia that is focused on care in the community and on maintaining and developing, what Kitwood (1997) called, the 'personhood' of the person with dementia. The Action Plan emphasises the need for the development of co-ordinated, multi-layered and well-resourced services, which are responsive to the individual needs of people with dementia and of those who care for them. The Plan also describes a model of best practice for the provision and planning of dementia care in Ireland that seeks to maximise the autonomy and capabilities of people with the disease.

6.14 ● The Action Plan sets out fully costed targets for the future care of people with dementia in the country. The main targets are as follows:

• increased public awareness about dementia;

• increase in early diagnosis through enhanced training and education for primary care workers;

• development of a case management model of integrated care;

• expansion of dedicated community-based services, for example, day care services, occupational therapists, community psychiatric nurses;

• expansion of dedicated old age psychiatry services;

• development of new and expanded psychosocial approaches to complement existing medical and neurological models of service delivery in the community and in residential care units;

- development of small-scale, appropriately designed, special residential care units; and

- development of new services for people with early onset dementia, including people with Down's Syndrome.

6.15 ● The Government's 2001 Health Strategy: *Quality and Fairness: A Health System for you* accepted the general thrust of the Action Plan and committed to its implementation over a seven year period. However, despite some improvements in recent years in enhanced training and education, increased at-home respite care, additional specialised dementia units and more old age psychiatry consultants, progress has been slow in implementing the Action Plan. The original Plan was modest in terms of its demands on the Exchequer, only requiring €20 million per year over a three-year period for its full implementation. This is equivalent to an annual grant of just over €600 per person with dementia. When presented in this way, the cost is minimal relative to the potential gains to be had.

Conclusion:
Prolonging Active Ageing for All

6.16 ● As outlined in Section 1 above, 'active ageing' stresses the importance of viewing ageing as a positive experience and one which optimises opportunities for health, participation and security in order to enhance quality of life as people age (World Health Organisation, 2002). In this Section of the report, the Team has highlighted the degree to which older people are not one homogenous group and that, while the majority live active and independent lives, some may have particular vulnerabilities and additional needs.

6.17 ● The Team emphasises the importance of active aging for all, not just for those who are most active or independent. In formulating policy, planning and delivering services for vulnerable older people, the principles and objectives of active aging need to be observed. Moreover, enhancing and prolonging people's social participation as they age is a core value that should inform action and secure a measured outcome. For those who are homeless or leaving institutional care, for example, this may mean providing supportive environments which, over time, actively encourage greater independence and autonomy. For those who are isolated, it means being innovative and flexible in responding to that situation. The Summerhill Active Retirement Group is an example of the valuable impact community-based groups can have on people's quality of life. For those who are vulnerable due to a disability, active ageing policy challenges us, as a society, to overcome the particular barriers to their participation in society.

6.18 ● In the next Section of the report, the Team stresses the importance of setting and achieving quality standards of care.

VII

Enhancing Quality of Care and Quality of Life

Introduction

7.1 ● In this Section of the report, the Team focuses on the importance of measuring the outcomes of policies and of ensuring that the best outcomes for older people are achieved. Two specific areas are covered. The first relates to quality of care and asks: what are the dimensions of good quality care for older people and how could we move towards becoming a world leader in this regard? The second area is in relation to healthy ageing, which is about extending the quantity and quality of life. The Team recognises that some progress has been made in recent years in both of these areas, but that more concerted effort is now required if the desired outcomes are to be achieved.

Quality of Care: Identifying Key Elements

7.2 ● Considerable financial resources have been invested in care for older people, both from public funding and from individuals and families. It is a big, and growing, business. But how do we know that the money being spent is achieving the best outcomes possible for older people, their families and society generally? What is an acceptable standard and what are the cost implications of reaching this standard?

7.3 ● There have been a number of concerns raised recently about standards in relation to some nursing homes. It is not appropriate for the Team to comment on individual care settings, and it is not in a position to comment on current overall standards in this sector; nor is it in a position to comment on the overall standards reached in community care settings. The systematic data needed to make such judgements are not available. What we do know from the research and from the written submissions received by the Team and from the Team's visits and consultations is that there are currently some very good care settings operating but others are in need of major and urgent improvement. What is also clear is that quality of care is about more than objective standards, such as buildings, facilities and staff ratios, etc.; but it also includes the context of care, or how people experience the service (O'Connor and Walsh, 1986, Murphy *et al*, forthcoming). A meaningful measurement of quality of care, therefore, must involve on-going consultation with service users.

7.4 ● The Health (Nursing Homes) Act, 1990 provides the legislative base for current standards in nursing homes (excluding the statutory sector). There is general agreement that these standards now need to be updated and modernised. The National Health Strategy *Quality and Fairness: A Health System for You (2001)* identified quality as a key principle and argued that it should be embedded in the health system through comprehensive and co-ordinated national and local programmes. It stated that quality in health means that evidence-based standards are set in partnership with consumers and are externally validated and that continuous improvement is valued. It also made two commitments in relation to the standard of health services for older people: firstly, that the remit of the Social Services Inspectorate would be extended to include residential care for older people and secondly, that national standards for community and long-term residential care of older people would be prepared.

7.5 ● The development of quality standards for older people's residential services is in keeping with the general shift towards care service improvement for other groups, for example:

- residential care services for children and young people (up to 18 years of age) – provided by the Social Services Inspectorate;

- residential care services for the provision of mental health services – provided by the Mental Health Commission; and

- residential care services for the provision of disability services – under preparation by the National Disability Authority.

7.6 ● The Irish Health Services Accreditation Board (IHSAB), which was established in 2002 to operate accreditation programmes for hospitals and other providers of health services, has expanded its accreditation scheme, on a pilot basis, to residential services including HSE care homes and hospitals for older people, HSE welfare homes, HSE district and community hospitals, voluntary care homes, private nursing homes, respite centres, related day care units, rehabilitation units and convalescent homes. Accreditation provides participating organisations with the process to assess their performance against standards of excellence and to determine what they are doing well and to identify areas for improvement. The system is based on a quality and safety framework that incorporates all aspects of service delivery. The process itself involves:

- self-assessment against internationally validated standards of excellence;

- peer and service user review survey;

- accreditation award decision; and

- continuous assessment.

7.7 ● The areas covered by the Scheme are grouped into five main categories, namely:

- **LEADERSHIP AND PARTNERSHIP** – covering governance, management and collaborative performance.

- **CARE/SERVICE** – focus on the provision of health care and /or services to patients/clients.

- **ENVIRONMENT AND FACILITIES MANAGEMENT** – covers the planning, development and maintenance of the building and equipment, infection control and waste management.

- **HUMAN RESOURCE MANAGEMENT** – provides the basis for an organisation to assess and evaluate its performance with respect to its staff.

- **INFORMATION MANAGEMENT** – relates to the management of information across the organisation.

  The project is on target for completion at the end of this October. The resulting outcome will be a set of standards and the associated accreditation process will then be available.

7.8 ● The Health Information and Quality Authority was established on an interim based in March 2005 and a Bill to establish it on a statutory basis is intended to be published later in the year. It will promote evidence-based delivery of high-quality health and personal social services and will have responsibility for:

- Developing health information systems;

- Promoting and implementing structured programmes of quality assurance;

- Reviewing and reporting on selected sets of services;

- Overseeing accreditation; and

- Developing health technology assessment.

7.9 ● At regional and local levels, there are a number of initiatives underway to improve the quality of care to older people in residential settings; however, these initiatives are not formally linked to each other and are patchy in coverage. The Essence of Care process, a patient-focused quality initiative, provides a framework for some of this work. It sets nine benchmark areas in relation to:

- privacy and dignity;
- food and nutrition;
- record keeping;
- continence;
- personal and oral hygiene;

- pressure ulcers;

- principles of self-care;

- safety; and

- communication.

7.10 ● Another recent initiative in this area is the Ten Steps to Healthy Ageing, developed by the National Council on Ageing and Older People and the Health Promoting Hospitals Network in Ireland to support healthy ageing best practice in residential care facilities. Details are given in Box 7.1 below.

Box 7.1

Ten Steps to Healthy Ageing

This is a joint initiative developed by the National Council on Ageing and Older People and the Health Promoting Hospitals Network in Ireland. Launched in January 2005, it will run in residential care facilities for older people and aims to heighten their health promotion capacity and impact. It has three key elements: i) person-centred care; ii), creating a positive working environment for those in care provision; and iii) creating a more family friendly environment. The ten steps are:

- **CONSULTATION** – residents identify their five most important aspects of their lives

- **HEALTH PROMOTION POLICY** – personalised policy developed

- **POLICY TO PRACTICE** – structure to assist and support best practice initiated

- **CHOICE** – residents involvement in decision-making and daily activity choices

- **INFORMATION PRACTICES** – effective communication process established

- **PERSONAL SPACE AND BELONGINGS** – individuality of all residents recognised

- **INDEPENDENCE** – autonomy of residents protected

- **LIFESTYLE** – healthy lifestyle choices of residents developed

- **HEALTHY STAFF** – staff development and training

- **FAMILY-FRIENDLY** – residents' continued involvement in family and community activities encouraged.

An evaluation of the initiative will be undertaken.

7.11 ● This focus on standards of care services for older people in residential care is to be welcomed. It is important, however, that the setting and measurement of standards are co-ordinated at a national level to ensure that there is consistency across different sites and to avoid duplication of effort and 're-inventing the wheel'. It is also important that advancement in the standards setting in residential sites is matched by quality initiatives in community services, for example: in relation to Day Care centres, the Home Help services and Meals on Wheels service, etc.

7.12 ● The Team considered that care standards for older people should be:

- comprehensive and be considered valid by and meaningful to service providers and users;

- mindful of the key role of care staff;

- built on existing protocols and drawn from best practice;

- developed and renewed in partnership with key stakeholders (older people and their families, services providers, etc);

- supported in a consistent way across HSE regions,

- measurable, both quantitatively and qualitatively, and the results publicly available to encourage choice and transparency;

- conducted by both specialists and lay persons;

- applied to both the public and private sectors;

- developed for both community and residential/institutional settings;

- viewed as a way of continuous improvement;

- informed by a consideration of the staffing implications, both overall and skills mix required to deliver a high quality service; and

- consistent across different categories or groups, for example, 'older people' and 'disabled'.

7.13 ● Quality of care is a key determinant of quality of life. It is inevitable that there will be differences in the quality of care in different settings. Environmental factors may play some part in explaining this difference. For example, privacy is very difficult to maintain in large wards and lack of adequate bathroom facilities reduce people's choices and independence. The continued improvement in the standard of accommodation, in both community and in long-stay settings, is important in raising the general quality of life of older people. High quality care, however, can be evident even in poor environmental settings, the key ingredient being high quality staff. Without this, quality of care cannot be achieved. Aspects of this element of quality of care will be difficult to regulate, however – staff morale and cohesiveness, staff-older person interactions, management leadership, the implementation of care ethos, for instance.

7.14 ● The key enabler in moving forward on the implementation of care standards is the extension of the remit of the Social Services Inspectorate to include residential care for older people, as committed to the Health Strategy, *Quality and Fairness: A Health System for You.*

The Team recommends that:

- the remit of the Social Services Inspectorate should be extended on a statutory basis to include all care settings for older people (residential, community and home-based; private, State or community/voluntary provision), with the necessary staff and financial resources;

- inspectors should be adequately trained and inspection findings should be published;

- there should be sanctions for non-compliance with standards;

- the principles of autonomy, empowerment and person-centredness should inform the development and implementation of the standards;

- standards should be clear, adequate and agreed, and developed in consultation with users;

- the Department of Health and Children should develop policy in relation to standards of care for older people in acute hospital settings;

- proactive development of higher standards is required to further move care towards quality of life measures; and

- standards should be developed and applied across all service levels – from front line service delivery, organisation of care, planning/integration and strategic development.

Enhancing Quality of Life in Community and Residential Care

7.15 ● Enhancing the quality of life of older people in different settings should be a key policy priority. In Section 1, the Team outlined how quality of life is related to health, well-being and general life satisfaction and personal development. Irish–based research indicates that older people's quality of life is generally good – many report excellent or good general health, few report loneliness, social networks are strong, and few feel that they have to go without things because of lack of money (Garavan *et al*, 2001;Treacy, *et al*, 2004; Latye, *et al*, 1999). But while ageing brings with it new opportunities and challenges, it also requires adjustments to manage these changes. A person's ability to adapt will depend not only on society's attitudes to ageing but also on their own previous life history and access to resources.

7.16 ● Research from the UK has stressed the importance of interdependence to achieving a 'good' old age (Godfrey, *et al*, 2004). This has many different facets – wanting to be part of a community where people care for and look out for each other, at the same time not wanting to be a burden on others but to be independent and being able to maintain reciprocity in relationships. In short, successful ageing is about being able to give to and receive from others emotional, social and practical support. It requires understanding and action at the following three levels:

- **INDIVIDUAL** – services and supports should open up opportunities for self-expression and engagement in social relationships and activities, provide practical, social and emotional support in coming to terms with managing life changes and offer assistance with dealing with the 'daily hassles' that constrain people's lives.

- **NEIGHBOURHOOD OR COMMUNITY LEVEL** – environments should be safe, secure and easily negotiated, as well as the integration of older people into decision-making structures and systems to effect positive change.

- **SOCIETAL LEVEL** – actions to reduce inequalities and changes in attitudes and values that are discriminatory and that devalue ageing (Godfrey, *et al*, 2004).

7.17 ● The following factors provide a framework for thinking about this complex area:

- **SUBJECTIVE ASSESSMENT** – asking people what is critical to their quality of life;

- **PHYSICAL ENVIRONMENT** – eg. housing, access to shops;

- **SOCIAL ENVIRONMENT** – eg. connectiveness to family and social networks;

- **SOCIO-ECONOMIC FACTORS** – eg. incomes, standards of living;

- **CULTURAL FACTORS** – eg. gender, age, ethnic backgrounds;

- **HEALTH STATUS** – eg. physical, mental wellbeing;

- **PERSONALITY** – eg. attitudes, morale, life satisfaction; and

- **PERSONAL AUTONOMY** – eg. independence, ability to make choices, etc. (Bond, *et al*, 2004).

7.18 ● The importance of interdependence for those living in the community also holds true for those in residential settings. In Section 5 of the Report, the Team recommended that residential care be recast to have a stronger focus on maintaining or regaining older people's independence. But it is equally important that this care should be of a high standard, and research has identified the following as key dimensions:

- A person's sense of self should be preserved by, for example, involving them in decisions, respecting privacy, encouraging independence, self-expression, maintaining clothes and personal belongings.

• The care environment and care ethos must be flexible, for example, a homely atmosphere, person-centred routines, encouragement of residence committees, staff training.

• People's links to the community, their social networks and family should be preserved; for example flexible visiting times, regular trips out, links to community activities, access to community therapy services.

• Programmes of activities (crafts, therapies, games, etc) should be meaningful and purposeful, and older people themselves should take part in planning and arranging these activities (*Age and Opportunity*, 2003; Murphy, forthcoming).

7.19 ● An important aspect of this discussion about increasing older people's independence, choice and autonomy is that of risk and risk taking. A balance has to be struck between risk and autonomy and opportunity. Kane (2001) put it well when she wrote:

"Older people may prefer the best health and safety outcomes possible that are consistent with a meaningful quality of life rather than the best quality of life that is consistent with health and safety." (Kane, 2001 p.293-304)

To be meaningful, this balance has to be struck in partnership with older people and their families.

Setting Healthy Ageing Targets

7.20 ● 'Healthy ageing' is the term used to describe health promotion policies for older people. It is concerned primarily with increasing the quantity and quality of life of older people and implies a focus on the maintenance of health, often through life style choices and preventative measures. In keeping with international experience that health promotion can have positive impacts on older people's health, a Healthy Ageing Programme has been operating here in Ireland since the late 1990s with the publication of *Adding Years to Life and Life to Years: A Health Promotion Strategy for Older People* (Brenner and Shelly, 1998). It has three main objectives:

• to improve life expectancy at age 65 and beyond (recent data shows an increase in life expectancy but we are still below the EU 25 average);

• to improve the health status of people aged 65 and beyond; and

• to improve the lives and autonomy of older people who are already affected by illness and impairment.

The Programme has three strands: firstly, the development of the health promotion strategy; secondly, the development of an information and support network for promoting health, welfare and autonomy; and thirdly the identification of models of good practice. Four health promotion areas were identified (with twenty-four goals), namely:

- **Specific disorders, accidents and suicide** – goals covered: cardiovascular disease, cancer, respiratory diseases, diabetes, musculoskeletal disorders, Parkinson's disease and multiple sclerosis, hearing and visual impairment, dental and oral disorders, foot disorders, incontinence, accidents, mental disorders, suicides, mediation awareness;

- **lifestyle** – goals related to: smoking, physical activity and alcohol;

- **physical environment** – goals included: housing, security, violence and abuse, transport, atmosphere and sunlight, water; and

- **social environment** – goals related to: attitudes, retirement income, social interaction, carers and sexuality.

Of the twenty-four goals identified, four had specific targets attached to them (namely, cardiovascular disease, cancer, accidents and smoking).

7.21 ● A survey of over 300 healthy ageing projects around the country (O'Shea, 2003) found that almost half (45 per cent) were social in nature, including social interaction, public attitudes, retirement issues and income support; while a further one in five (20 per cent) focused on behavioural and lifestyle issues, including physical activities, smoking, drinking, nutrition and diet. Projects covering the physical environment of older people (housing, transport, security, etc) accounted for 17 per cent of projects, while only 10 per cent focused on specific diseases (heart disease, cancer, mental disorders, arthritis, etc) and 6 per cent focused on accidents and suicides. These activities took place in a wide variety of settings, including day care centres (16 per cent), active retirement groups (15 per cent), in older people's homes (10 per cent) and in public long-stay care settings (10 per cent). The absence of projects in General Practitioner primary care settings (3 per cent) and the poor representation of projects in the housing and transport sectors (2 per cent respectively) were noted by O'Shea. When asked to prioritise areas to develop should additional funding become available, the following areas were ranked as the top five:

  (i) social interaction and integration;

  (ii) promotion of better attitudes to old age in society;

  (iii) mental health problems;

  (iv) stroke prevention; and

  (v) personal/creative development of older people.

Those living alone, the homeless and those in deprived economic circumstances and rural older people were ranked as the top four categories of older people to receive additional funding, should it become available.

7.22 ● In the on-going development of the Healthy Ageing Strategy, the Team considers that the following points should receive attention:

- greater attention needs to be given to addressing ageism as a barrier to healthy and successful ageing (see Section 2);

- healthy ageing priorities should be set in partnership with a wide range of stakeholders;

- the goals of healthy ageing should be prioritised, targets set, progress measured and monitored;

- there should be a balance between medical and social aspects of healthy ageing, and linkages made between different healthy ageing programmes;

- innovation and experimentation among local and voluntary groups should be supported, and best practice should be sustained and disseminated;

- a dedicated health promotion budget for older people should be set;

- the promotion of health for older people is a multi-Departmental and muti-sector issue.

Conclusion

7.23 ● In this Section of the report the Team has stressed the importance of adopting evidence-based policy-making approaches and of focusing on the ultimate goal of better quality of life and quality of care for older people as a key policy objective. The approach is part of the mind-set change which the Team advocates. In the next, and final Section of the report, the Team brings together and sets out its views and recommendations on the priority areas for change.

VIII

Delivering Change: Implementation

Opportunities for Change

8.1 ● In this report, we have presented a vision of care which places a high value on older people's independence, autonomy and choice. The time is right for the reform of current approaches, taking into account that:

• There are increasing numbers of older people, the majority of whom lead independent and active community lives and want to remain that way for as long as possible.

• Older people's expectations are changing in line with those of the general society towards a requirement for high quality, responsive services.

• The level and consistency of informal or family care in the home which was available to older people in the past will not be there to the same degree in the future.

• There is a growing body of evidence that preventative approaches are more efficient and effective, with better outcomes for older people, than services which only react when a crisis point is reached.

• The establishment of the HSE provides an opportunity to implement new ways of thinking and new approaches.

A New Vision of Care for Older People

8.2 ● At the root of this new approach is a different mind-set to inform service planning and delivery. This should be based on maintaining or restoring older people's independence, in all settings, and ensuring they are able to exercise their own choices to the utmost. Consulting with older people about what they want and using a partnership approach in response is crucial to achieving these choices. This is a culture that values enabling environments, which anticipates changing needs throughout the life cycle and facilitates people to remain living where they want to for as long as possible. It is one where a range of high-quality, core services is available to older people when needed; where information on available services and supports is easy to access; where services dovetail with each other to deliver a whole package instead of older people having to rely on word-of-mouth and chance to access fragmented and compartmentalised responses. This approach values innovation and finding new ways of doing things on an ongoing basis, drawing on the latest research and best practice models.

8.3 ● In this final Section of the report, we focus on delivering change to achieve this vision. The Team is conscious that implementation to date has been slow and patchy in this policy area. At the same time, it acknowledges that much good work is already being done, but that this often needs to be consolidated and placed within a more strategic framework.

Priorities for Change

8.4 ● Throughout this report, we have reiterated a vision of how care services for older people might better respond to older people's needs and preferences. Here, we outline the next steps in translating this vision towards the reality of a more person-centred service model. This will require prioritising. During its consultations and visits, the Team was conscious of the considerable amount of energy, activity and effort which is evident on a day-to-day basis in caring for older people in different settings and in different circumstances. The Team were also very aware of the contribution which older people themselves make to society and the imperative that this be respected and valued. The Team puts forward the following over-arching policy recommendations as priority areas for action:

• plan positively for an ageing population;

• root out ageism;

• clarify entitlement;

• strengthen co-ordination;

• develop person-centred needs assessment;

• implement care and case management;

• improve standards of care;

• support homecare; and

• maintain and develop housing stock.

8.5 ● The Team has made detailed recommendations throughout the report, which are collated in the Executive Summary, to implement a programme of change to address these priorities. The Team is clear that these changes will have financial implications. However, there are cost implications attached to remaining in the status quo, and substantial benefits from shifting our focus to invest more in community responses. This shift is possible given:

• our relatively low level of social expenditure on services for older people relative to our wealth and stage of development;

• forecasts of continued economic growth and manageable demographic changes;

- current spending being biased towards institutional responses, which are not always needed or the older person's preference; and

- research which indicates positive outcomes from investment in community-based services, particularly if they are planned and delivered in a strategic way.

Key Actors

8.6 ● Key actors are required to champion the implementation of this report. Where possible, we have identified these when making recommendations.

8.7 ● It is also important that the voices of older people are heard, at the national priority policy-setting level and also at the individual needs-assessment level. In Sections 1 and 5, the Team emphasised the importance of making issues affecting older people more central to national and local planning and delivery and enhancing the capacity of organisations representing older people's interests.

8.8 ● At an individual level, the Team has also stressed the importance of consulting with older people in the planning and delivery of services. It is particularly important that those who are vulnerable or at high risk of marginalisation are included in this process. At an individual level, advocates can play a crucial role in ensuring that the views and wishes of the older person are heard and respected.

Setting Targets and Monitoring Progress

8.9 ● The value of setting targets for change is clear. One need only look to the experience of the National Anti-Poverty Strategy (NAPS), which in 1997 set ambitious targets to substantially reduce poverty and social exclusion over a ten-year period. In the intervening time, the NAPS targets have acted as a basis to monitor progress and to maintain poverty to the fore in the policy-making agenda and also new targets have been added as our understanding of the dynamic of this approach has deepened.

8.10 ● In addition to setting targets it is also important that progress is actively monitored. Throughout this report, the need for more sophisticated information structures and information flows about people's needs, services and outcomes has been stressed. This would allow for more accurate accounting and evaluation frameworks to be developed to improve the quality of care and quality of life of older people. Data are needed at:

- an individual level, for example through the holistic and unified needs-assessment process the Team recommends;

- a programme level, in terms of efficiency and effectiveness; and

- planning and policy levels, to ensure that policy objectives are achieved.

Data are also required to track the impact of ageing and the ageing process over time, and to help inform our understanding of the determinants of successful ageing.

A Dynamic Model of Ageing

8.11 ● In conclusion, the Team emphasises the need to view ageing in a more dynamic way, one which does not automatically equate ageing with increased dependency, but with diversity. This diversity requires us to shift to a more person-centred approach, which is vital if we are to respond successfully to the emerging social and economic contexts outlined in this report.

8.12 ● Changing our approach to care for older people will have many positive spin-offs for older people themselves, by enhancing quality of life, but will also benefit society by increasing and sustaining older people's ability to participate and contribute to society, through family, community or workplace.

Annexes

Annex 1   References

Age and Opportunity (2003) *Home from Home? The Views of Residents on Social Gain and Quality of Life. A Study in Three Care Centres for Older People.* Dublin: Age and Opportunity.

Barrett, A. and Bergin, A. (2005) 'Assessing Age-Related Pressures on the Public Finances 2005 to 2050 in Callan, T., Doris, A., Barrett, A., Bergin, A., Coleman, K., McHale, J., Morgenroth, E., and Walsh, J., *Budget Perspectives 2006.* Dublin: Economic and Social Research Institute.

Bergin, A., Cullen, J., Duffy, D., Fitz Gerald, J. Kearney, D, and McCoy, D. (2003) *Medium term review: 2003 – 2010.* Dublin: Economic and Social Research Institute.

Bond, J. and Corner, L. (2004) *Quality of Life and Older People.* Milton Keynes: Open University Press.

Brenner, H. and Shelley, E. (1998) *Adding Years to Life and Life to Years: A Health Promotion Strategy for Older People.* Report Number 50. Dublin: National Council on Ageing and Older People.

Bytheway, B. (1995) *Ageism.* Buckingham: The Open University Press.

Central Statistics Office (2004) *Census of Population 2002 – Volume 10 Disability and Carers.* Dublin: Stationery Office

Challis, D. (2002) 'Care Management: Who Needs it? What Makes it Work? Lessons from International Experience' in Quill, S. (Editor) *Conference Proceedings: Towards Care Management in Ireland.* Report Number 71. Dublin: National Council on Ageing and Older People.

CHOICE Programme (2002) *Choice Survey: Sligo/Leitrim Results.* North Western Health Board.

CHOICE Programme (2003) *Policy for Services for Older People.* North Western Health Board.

Commonwealth Department of Health and Ageing (2003) *A New Strategy for Community Care Consultation Paper.* Australia.

Conboy, P. (Editor) (2002) *Assessment of Older People's Health and Social Care Needs and Preferences: Conference Proceedings.* Report Number 72. National Council on Ageing and Older People.

Connell P. and Pringle, D. (2004) *Population Ageing in Ireland Projections 2002 – 2021.* Report Number 81. Dublin: National Council on Ageing and Older People.

Co-ordinating Group of Secretaries (1996) *Second Report to Government of the Co-ordinating Group of Secretaries: A Programme of Change for the Irish Civil Service.* Dublin: Stationery Office.

Crowley, N. (2005) 'Equality Competences in Service Provision' *National Conference: Towards an Age-friendly Society.* www.ncaop.ie

Cullen, K. Delaney, S. Duff, P. (2004) *Caring, Working and Public Policy* Dublin: The Equality Authority.

Delaney, S., Garavan, R., McGee, H., and Tynan, A. (2001) *Care and Case Management for Older People in Ireland: An Outline of Current Status and a Best Practice Model for Service Development.* Report Number 66. Dublin: National Council on Ageing and Older People.

Department of the Environment, Heritage and Local Government (2004) *Building Regulations 2000, Technical Guidance Document M: Access for People with Disabilities.* Dublin: Stationery Office.

Department of the Environment, Heritage and Local Government (2002) *Housing Statistics Bulletin, September Quarter 2002.* Dublin: Stationery Office.

Department of Health and Children (2002) *Your Views about Health: Report on Consultation. Quality and Fairness – A Health System for You: Health Strategy.* Dublin: Department of Health and Children.

Department of Health and Children (2001) *Primary Care: A New Direction. Quality and Fairness – A Health System for You: Health Strategy.* Dublin: Department of Health and Children.

Department of Health and Children (2001) *Quality and Fairness – A Health System for You: Health Strategy.* Dublin: Department of Health and Children.

Department of the Taoiseach (2003) *Sustaining Progress: Social Partnership Agreement 2003 – 2005.* Dublin: Stationery Office

Elkan, R, Kendrick, D. Dewey, M. Hewitt, M. Robinson, J. Blair, M. Williams, D. and Brummell, K. (2001) 'Effectiveness of home based support for older people: systematic review and meta-analysis' *British Medical Journal* Volume 323, 29 September 2001pp1-9.

Fitzpatrick Associates (2004) *External Evaluation of the Rural Transport Initiative* Dublin: Area Development Management Ltd.

Garavan, R. Winder, R. and McGee, H. (2001) *Health and Social Services for Older People (HeSSOP): Consulting Older People on Health and Social Services: A Survey of Service Use, Experiences and Needs.* Report Number 64. Dublin: National Council on Ageing and Older People.

Godfrey, M., Townsend, J. and Denby, T. (2004) *Building a Good Life for Older People in Local Communities: The Experience of Ageing in Time and Place.* York: Joseph Rowntree Foundation.

Health Service Executive East Coast Area (2005) *Slán Abhaile: The Pilot Phase.*

Houses of the Oireachtas Joint Committee on Social and Family Affairs (2003) *Report on the Position of Full-time Carers: First Report*. Dublin: Houses of the Oireachtas. PRN No 1378

Huber, B. (2005) 'Images of Ageing: Policy Considerations for an Age-Friendly Society' *National Conference: Towards an Age-Friendly Society in Ireland* www.ncaop.ie

Inter-Departmental Group on the Needs of Older People (2004) *Progress Report: April 2004*. Dublin: Department of Health and Children.

Irish Council for Social Housing (2005) *An Overlooked Option in Caring of the Elderly: A Report on Sheltered and Group Housing Provided by Housing Associations in Ireland*. Dublin: Irish Council for Social Housing.

Joseph Rowntree Foundation Task Group on Housing, Money and Care for Older People (2003) *Quality of Life for Older People: From Welfare to Well-being*. York: Joseph Rowntree Foundation.

Joseph Rowntree Foundation (2003) *Welfare and Well-being: Planning for an Ageing Society*. York: Joseph Rowntree Foundation.

Kane, R.A. (2001) 'Long-term Care and a Good Quality of Life: Bringing Them Closer Together' *Gerontologist*. Vol. 41 No. 3 pp293 – 304.

Kitwood, T. (1997) 'Personhood, dementia and dementia care.' In S. Hunter (ed.) *Dementia: Challenges and New Directions*. London: Jessica Kingsley Publications.

Layte, R. Fahey, T. and Whelan, C. (1999) *Income, Deprivation and Well-Being Among Older Irish People*. Report Number 55. Dublin: National Council on Ageing and Older People.

McAteer, D. and Roberts, B. (2005) *Involving Rural Populations in Improving Their Health and Wellbeing*. Summerhill Active Retirement Group.

McCoy, R., Duffy, D., Bergin, A., Garrett, S., and McCarthy, Y. (2005) *Quarterly Economic Commentary: Summer 2005*. Dublin: Economic and Social Research Institute.

McGlone, E. and Fitzgerald, F. (2005) *Perceptions of Ageism in Health and Social Services in Ireland*. Report Number 85. Dublin: National Council on Ageing and Older People.

Mercer Limited (2003) *Study to Examine the Future Financing of Long-term Care in Ireland*. Dublin: Department of Social and Family Affairs.

Mullen, P (2002) *The Imaginary Time Bomb: Why an Ageing Population is Not a Social Problem*. London: I.B. Tauris Publishers.

Murphy, K. (forthcoming) *Quality of Life for Older People in Long-stay Care*. National University of Ireland, Galway.

National Cancer Registry Ireland (2005) *Cancer in Ireland 1994 – 2001: A report from the National Cancer Registry*. Cork.

National Council for the Elderly (1992) *Co-ordinating Services for the Elderly at Local Level: Swimming Against the Tide. A Report on Two Pilot Projects*. Report Number 23a. Dublin: National Council for the Elderly.

National Council on Ageing and Older People (2005) *An Age-friendly Society: A Position Statement*. Dublin: National Council on Ageing and Older People.

National Economic and Social Council (2005) *The Developmental Welfare State*. Dublin: National Economic and Social Council.

National Economic and Social Council (2004) *Housing in Ireland: Performance and Policy*. Dublin: National Economic and Social Council.

National Economic and Social Forum (2004) *Fourth Periodic Report on the Work of the NESF*. Report Number 30. Dublin: National Economic and Social Forum.

National Economic and Social Forum (2003) *Equality Policies for Older People: Implementation Issues*. Report Number 29. Dublin: National Economic and Social Forum.

National Economic and Social Forum (2003) *Equality Policies for Lesbian, Gay and Bisexual People: Implementation Issues*. Report Number 27. Dublin: Stationery Office.

National Economic and Social Forum (2002) *A Strategic Policy Framework for Equality Issues*. Report Number 23. Dublin: Stationery Office.

O'Connor, J. and Walsh, M. (1986) *It's Our Home: The Quality of Life in Private and Voluntary Nursing Homes*. Dublin: National Council for the Aged.

O'Connor, S. and Dowds, L. (2005) '*Ageism and Attitudes to Older People in the Republic of Ireland: Report of ARK Survey, 2003*' in McGivern, Y. (Ed) *From Ageism to Age Equality: Addressing the Challenges*. Report Number 86. Dublin: National Council on Ageing and Older People.

Office of the Revenue Commissioners (2003) *Statistical Report*. Dublin: Offices of the Revenue Commissioners.

O'Loughlin, A and Duggan, J. (1998) *Abuse, Neglect and Mistreatment of Older People: An Exploratory Study*. Report Number 52. Dublin: National Council on Ageing and Older People.

O'Neill, D. Gibson, J. Mulpeter, K. (2001) 'Responding to Care Needs in Long-term Care' *Irish Medical Journal*. Volume 94. Number 3. March 2001.

Organisation for Economic Co-operation and Development (2005) *Long-term Care Policies for Older People*. Paris: OECD

O'Shea, E. (2004) *The Seniors Help Line: Older People Working for Older People. An Economic and Social Evaluation*. Summerhill Active Retirement Group.

O'Shea, E. (2003) *Review of the Nursing Home Subvention Scheme.* Dublin: Stationery Office.

O'Shea E. (2003) *Health Ageing in Ireland: Policy, Practice and Evaluation.* Report Number 77. Dublin: National Council on Ageing and Older People.

O'Shea, E. (2002) *Improving the Quality of Life of Elderly Persons in Situations of Dependency.* Strasbourg: Council of Europe.

O'Shea, E. (2002) *Review of the Nursing Home Subvention Scheme.* Dublin: Stationery Office.

O'Shea, E. and Hughes, J. (1995) *The Economics and Financing of Long-Term Care of the Elderly in Ireland.* Dublin: National Council for the Elderly.

PA Consulting Group (2002) *Evaluation of the Strategic Management Initiative.*

Ruddle, H. Donoghue, F. and R. Mulvihill (1997) *The Years Ahead Report: A Review of the Implementation of its Recommendations.* Report Number 48. Dublin: National Council on Ageing and Older People.

Shiely, F and Kelleher, C. (2004) *Older People in Ireland: A Profile of Health Status, Lifestyle and Socio-Economic Factors from SLÁN.* National Council on Ageing and Older People. Report No. 82.

The Carers Association (2005) *Towards a Family Carers Strategy.* Kilkenny: The Carers Association

Timonen, V (2004) *Evaluation of Homecare Grant Schemes in the NAHB and ECAHB.* Department of Social Studies, Trinity College Dublin.

Tracey, P. Butler, M, Byrne, A Drennan, J. Fealy,, G. Frase, K. and Irving, K. (2004) *Loneliness and Social Isolation Among Older Irish People.* Report Number 84. National Council on Ageing and Older People.

United Nations Development Programme (2005) *Human Development Report 2005: International Cooperation at a Crossroads: Aid, Trade and Security in an Unequal World.* New York: United Nations.

Williams, J and Gorby, S. (2002) *Counter In 2002: The Report of the Assessment of Homelessness in Dublin.* Dublin: Homeless Agency.

Williams, T. F. (1996) 'Geriatrics: perspectives on quality of life and care for older people'. In Spilker B. (ed) *Quality of Life and Pharma-economics in Clinical Trials.* 2nd edition, Philadelphia, PA, Lippincott-Raven.

Working Group on Elder Abuse (2002) *Protecting Our Future: Report of the Working Group on Elder Abuse.* Dublin: Government Publications.

Working Party on Services for the Elderly (1988) *The Years Ahead: A Policy for the Elderly.* Dublin: Stationery Office.

World Health Organisation (2002) *Active Ageing: A Policy Framework.* Geneva: World Health Organisation.

Annex 2　Terms of Reference for the Project Team

There is agreement that, by and large, older people want to live at home, that they should be able to do so and that the range of community-care options to support that choice needs to be extended. Any reform of the current system of resource allocation for dependent older people should, therefore, be part of a wider strategy of keeping older people living in the community, while retaining a strong capacity to meet long-term care needs within public and private long-stay care facilities.

The focus of the Team's work will be to examine the current set of choices available to older people in respect of health and social care in Ireland and to identify any gaps in the continuum of care that currently exist. All aspects of the lives of dependent elderly people will be considered with particular emphasis on:

— the positive contribution of older people and the need for their greater participation in defining policy;

— promoting positive ageing and independence and equity for older people in economic, social and cultural life, particularly the most vulnerable;

— separating dependency from situations of dependency for older people;

— examining current resource allocation for older people in community and long-stay settings;

— promoting the social integration of dependent older people through the development of integrated primary and community care models, life adaptable accommodation, public transport, life-long learning, technology, etc;

— the legal dimensions, both in terms of a 'rights-based' approach and legislative barriers to greater community participation in care;

— encouraging various forms of solidarity (families, neighbours, communities, volunteers, statutory);

— exploring the meaning of quality of life for vulnerable older people in community and long-stay care settings, including people with dementia;

— examining the nature and process of policy formulation and policy implementation for older people; and

— the impact of age discrimination and how it should be tackled.

In undertaking the work, the Project Team will adopt a positive holistic view of ageing and later life, which stresses the importance of older people's full participation in economic, social and cultural life. The objective of the Project Team will be to nurture and develop inter-generational solidarity at the level of the family and State through dialogue and discussion among all of the social partners, including older people themselves.

Annex 3   Summary of Written Submissions Received

Introduction

In December 2004, the Project Team placed a call for written submissions on *Care for Older People* in the main national newspapers. 125 individuals and organisations with an interest in or experience of this area responded to this call. In a number of cases, organisations held focus group meetings with different groups of service users and staff to record their own experiences and views. This brought the total number of submissions received to 147.

A significant proportion of the submissions came from service providers working in a range of community and voluntary and health and social service settings. Submissions were also received from a number of individuals (including researchers, academics and older people themselves), as well as from local services, statutory bodies and universities. A list of the individuals and organisations who made submissions is provided at the end of this Annex.

In issuing the call for submissions, the Project Team highlighted the three core themes underpinning its work, namely:

— policy evaluation and obstacles to effective implementation;

— encouraging the participation and realising the potential of all older people; and

— the provision of the best services possible, particularly in relation to health and social services.

The focus of the Project Team's work on enhancing older people's care services and identifying any gaps in supporting the wishes of the majority of people to live at home was also highlighted in the call for submissions.

While some of the submissions gave attention to all of these issues, a significant proportion focused on a select number of them. Issues related to supporting older people who want to live at home were highlighted in the majority of them and this was closely followed by the development of health, community and social services for older people. Encouraging the participation of older people in various settings also featured strongly in the submissions. While many submissions focused on a range of issues related to care for older people, some of them concentrated on particular thematic areas (e.g. health and well-being), while others focused on the experiences of particular groups of older people (e.g. older people with disabilities).

The following is a summary of the main points raised in the submissions.

Older people in Ireland

Many submissions made reference to existing statistics on older people and drew attention to data which show that life expectancy in Ireland is one of the lowest in the EU. A range of factors was highlighted to explain these data, including low levels of service provision for older people in Ireland and the low levels of involvement of older people in the design and delivery of services which impact on them. In the vast majority of cases, it was felt that older people's voices are not heard, for example:

"People speak for older people instead of allowing them to speak for themselves. Ageism prohibits the development of services. Stereotyping and negative perceptions adversely affect services."

The impact of ageism and age discrimination on older people was highlighted in a significant number of the submissions received, for example:

"The care provided should be equitable but the danger of ageism, discrimination and arbitrary decision-making is high. The policy in at least one major acute hospital is that if a person over sixty-five, having suffered myocardial infraction (heart attack) attends the emergency department that person will be admitted to a medical ward rather

than to the Coronary Care Unit, therefore they are denied access to specialist care on the basis of their age alone."

It was felt that ageism is manifest in all sections of society and continues to have a particularly negative impact on the design and delivery of policies and services. One submission simply said:

"We would like to see a greater consensus emerging in public life about the fact that ageism and age discrimination exist and greater will to tackle it."

Here individuals and organisations expressed the need for policy-makers and service providers to distinguish between what they view as being appropriate for older people and what older people view as being appropriate for themselves. On this issue, one organisation noted the following:

"Even when much goodwill is in evidence toward the older people with whom they work, it can be expressed in quite disempowering terms with insufficient awareness of older people as active participants in their own care or of their rights to continue to shape their own futures, let alone of people who still have a contribution to make to society generally."

According to many of the submissions, tackling this issue requires a shift in mindset from one which views older people as passive citizens, for example:

"There is a required shift in mindset needed in terms of looking at the person and their contribution to society rather than they being perceived as a cost factor to the State."

In essence, it was felt that greater attention needs to be given to protecting the dignity and independence of older people and in this context, frequent reference was made to the need to promote 'positive' and 'healthy' ageing. Translating this to service provision, one submission noted that:

" ... 'healthy' ageing requires services that open up opportunities for self-expression and engagement in

social relationships and activities rather than one that treats people as totally passive recipients of services."

On this issue, another submission noted the following:

"For older people to have genuine dignity and independence may require that policy should aim not to provide 'care' but to facilitate 'independent living.' The notion of independent living fits with the concept of 'positive ageing' ... For the positive ageing of older people, therefore, it is important ... that the financing arrangements should be changed to make it easier for older people to remain living in the community ..."

As well as involving older people in policy-influencing opportunities, submissions stressed the need to increase the choices available to older people in general. In particular, it was felt that older people should have the power to choose the health, community and/or social care packages that best suit their individual needs. One submission summarised this as follows:

"We submit the principle that the people who know best what they need are the people themselves. [This] should be recognised as also applying to the older generation, so that a policy of active involvement of older people should be required in decision making, policy development and implementation of decisions related to them, and that this should be real and substantial and not mere tokenism."

In this context, many submissions called for the introduction of a more rights-based approach to service provision in Ireland which, it was felt, would lead to a more favourable environment for supporting the economic, social, personal and cultural development of older people. According to one submission:

"The government has also tended to side step the introduction of rights-based legislation such as a lack of implementation of a Charter of Rights for the Elderly devised by the Irish Congress of Trade Unions and the National Federation of Pensioner's Association."

Some submissions gave particular attention to the needs and rights of older women, noting that they are a particularly vulnerable group in our society both because of their longer life expectancy than men and the increased levels of poverty and ill-health associated with older age. A key concern for this group is the failure on the part of the state to award pension credits to women who have opted to work full-time in the home. On this issue, one submission had the following to say:

"It is imperative that older women should have economic independence, as a right. It is a national injustice that elderly women, who forfeited their careers to devote their "best years" to home making, are deprived of the independence and dignity of having a pension of their own."

Concern was also expressed about the needs of older people aged 65 years and over. One submission noted, for example, that the high morbidity of people in this age range is often due to their lifestyle, adding that "there is a severe limitation on the choices available to healthy, energetic people simply due to their age." It was noted that older people under 70 years who do not have a medical card have no entitlement to disability aids, even where these aids are required. Retirement was itself identified as a barrier to positive ageing for many older people, particularly people aged 65 years and over. According to one submission, for example:

"Retirement often operates as a process of both social and political exclusion, detaching older people from some of the main sources of political consciousness and channels of representation."

A number of submissions noted that retirement arrangements should be sufficiently flexible to accommodate people who wish to remain in employment and that appropriate provisions should be put in place to facilitate semi- and full retirement, including reduced working hours and relevant pre-retirement courses, where required.

Disability was identified as another obstacle facing a significant number of older people. Highlighting recent data, one submission noted

that approximately four out of ten people with a disability are aged 65 and over, comprising almost one-third of all those with a disability. It was further noted that close to two thirds of disabled people over 65 years experience more than one kind of disability or restriction, with the incidence of multiple restrictions rising with age. Among the priorities for older people with disabilities were the need for more accessible and affordable aids and adaptations, more disability-friendly home and built environments and a more comprehensive system of care. Calls were also made for the Departments of the Environment, Heritage and Local Government and Health and Children to develop a joint National Accommodation and Support Strategy and for improvements to the Disabled Person's Grant Scheme, in terms of funding and administration.

Submissions gave attention to the needs of older people with dementia, noting that approximately 40,000 people in Ireland have this illness. It was noted that older people who lose their decision-making ability are a particularly vulnerable group and it was felt that priority should be given to developing facilities for the initial and on-going assessment of people with memory loss to ensure early diagnosis and treatment. One submission stressed the need for further research into the psychosocial aspect of dementia, adding that:

" ... there is a need for increased dementia awareness and the creation of more dementia friendly environments in residential facilities. Appropriate units with a suitable environment and adequately trained staff are urgently required for persons with dementia."

Levels of social welfare pensions were also highlighted as a particular concern for older people. It was noted, for example, that incomes from pensions tend to be fixed at the time of retirement, with little or no means available to older people to increase them. For this reason, it was felt that a mechanism should be put in place to ensure that older people's pensions increase with general improvements in wages. On this issue, one submission noted the following:

"Social welfare benefits must be increased and linked automatically to increases in wage levels. A target of 34% of average industrial earnings was set by the National Pensions Policy Initiative. The Parliament is now calling for this recommendation to be implemented and to be further improved in future years until the target of 40% of average industrial earnings is reached. This will ensure that social welfare pensions are benchmarked against increases in earnings and general economic prosperity."

Current state of services and facilities for older people

The majority of submissions gave attention to describing the current state of services and facilities for older people in Ireland. A relatively high proportion noted that there have been a number of positive developments in recent years. Of these, the two most frequently mentioned developments included the home-help service and meals-on-wheels. The contribution made by day care and social centres was also highlighted, as was the provision of sheltered housing and community nursing homes. Concessions on TV licences and telephone charges, as well as the extension of the medical card, were noted as being particularly positive developments for people aged 70 years and over. However, while recognising the positive contributions that developments such as these have made to older people's lives, the submissions acknowledged their limitations, for example:

"Home Help is an excellent concept but there are not enough. Aids and appliances and assistive technology are very beneficial but there are budgetary constraints. Day Care Centres and Social Centres are great but need to be developed in more places and in various locations."

In essence, it was felt that there is considerable variation in the type of services and facilities available to older people across the country and that this is a major impediment to their overall quality of life. One submission put it as follows:

" ... many services are developed in a patchy and ad hoc manner which is problematic to an older person's ability to access same. Whereas there are unique localised geographical needs and solutions throughout the country, a person's place of residence should not determine the quality and extent of supports available."

This sentiment was a strong feature across the majority of submissions received. In general, considerable dissatisfaction was expressed in relation to the level, type and range of services and facilities available to older people in different geographical locations. Urban and rural variations were emphasised throughout, with a significant number of submissions highlighting the particular difficulties facing older people living in remote areas, for example:

"As has been said before, geography can be a crucial decider in who gets what, with huge variations in service provision, dementia services may be good in one area, stroke rehabilitation in another, hospital [care] in another, while palliative care may be accessible in another."

In summing up, one submission stated the following:

"Much lip service has been paid to provision of service to older people. We have many excellent policy documents outlining proposals and action plans for delivery of services which older people require to live their lives with dignity and with choice. We do not require any more of these documents. We need to update the statistical data for the growing numbers of older people and then we need to be provided with adequate funding and suitably qualified health and social care workers to assist older people, their carers and family to assist older people to live in their chosen environments with dignity, privacy and respect."

Other points relating to current services and facilities for older people focused on a number of distinct but interrelated areas, which are summarised as follows:

Cost, availability and quality of services

Frequent mention was made of the cost of care for older people. In particular, submissions referred to the high costs associated with hospital care, primary care and nursing home care. Routine health examinations were also considered to be costly, especially for older people who are living on low pensions and for those who do not quality for a medical card. Many submissions noted that older people neglect their health because of the costs attached to G.P. visits and medication.

The cost-related difficulties in providing services for older people were also highlighted, with one submission noting the following:

"Implementing the best services possible in relation to social services isn't a problem. Obtaining the funds to carry out the services is the obstacle."

Serious concerns were raised about the availability of services. In particular, it was felt that services are not always available at times that are suitable to older people. A high proportion of the submissions noted that services are generally not provided at the weekends and that there is a clear gap in service provision during bank holiday and Christmas periods. One submission simply noted that:

"24 hour/7 day a week community services are currently unavailable and there is no evidence of a commitment or a desire to provide same."

The lack of an 'on-call service' in certain locations (particularly for people with high dependencies), the limited availability of breast screening in particular regions, and the absence of nursing home care in various areas were also identified as key concerns. In addition, reference was made to the limited availability of physiotherapy and occupational therapy, regular day care places, respite care, and counselling services (especially bereavement counselling).

Both the high costs and limited availability of existing services and facilities were identified as compromising the overall quality of service provision for older people, with the result that "services are often reactive, only dealing with acute and chronic problems rather than prevention and health promotion."

In general, it was felt that services are largely focused on meeting the health needs of older people. The importance of broadening out this focus was summed up in the following way in one of the submissions received:

"Yes traditional care services are important, we need physiotherapists, occupational therapists, nurses, medical aids and devices etc. but ... other aspects of care are just as important, those elements that are non traditional or novel, such as community delivered health initiatives, provision of information in relation to health, rights, entitlements etc, capacity building, raising awareness, tackling policy issues, lifelong learning activities, confidence building, raising esteem, community development projects, social interactions etc."

Access to services

Access to services for older people was considered to be compromised by inadequate transportation facilities, particularly in rural areas. It was noted that facilities for older people are heavily concentrated in developed urban areas which are often inaccessible to older people living in remote towns and villages. One submission put it as follows:

"Lack of transport in certain isolated rural areas is seriously problematic. For example, to go to Tralee for an X-ray etc. from Dingle is 'a nightmare'."

Access to services for older people is also affected by the high level of demands being placed on the limited services available. One submission drew on the experiences of medical card holders to illustrate this problem:

"Holders of medical cards are entitled to certain services but are prevented from receiving their entitlements because the demand for many services is greater than supply e.g. there is a waiting list of

seven months for chiropody treatment in the Southern Health Board Region of Cork City. The State insists on providing the service itself and fails. If private chiropodists were contracted to service public patients there would be no waiting lists."

Primary care and hospital care

Here it was noted that doctors are not always available to meet older people at home and that many require older people to visit their offices, which is not always possible. It was also felt that there are too few public health nurses, with "work overload preventing them from paying more regular visits." Another key concern was identified as the lack of development and implementation in relation to the Primary Care Strategy.

It was generally felt that hospital care falls considerably short of the standard required by older people. Key concerns related to the shortage of hospital beds and the length of time spent waiting for hospital treatments. A number of submissions also raised questions about the overall quality of care for older people in acute hospitals, stating that there is a general lack of understanding of their specific needs and entitlements.

Community, home and social care

A common point of concern across many submissions was the Government's failure to both advance and fund many recent policies for older people and in particular, its failure to implement policy recommendations on home and community services. On this issue, one submission noted that:

"Some of the commitments in the 1994 Health Strategy in relation to older people have not been implemented. There is a need to implement the following, - the drawing up of national guidelines and legislation to deal with community care services; - the publication of a charter of rights in relation to older people."

It was felt that commitments in relation to clarifying entitlements to community care services and developing an integrated approach to care planning for older people should be fully implemented.

Submissions observed that care services for older people largely focus on personal and home support services, with little consideration given to the emotional and social needs of older people. Specifically:

"When one considers the high numbers of people over 65 and even more over 70 who live alone, the development of social and activity based services to serve this need is essential. These services could include assisting people to go out for a walk, shopping, to the bank, playing a game of cards, doing the crossword, reading a book to a person. Consideration should be given to the actual provision of such services in terms of time and financial resources as ... [s]uch services significantly improve quality of life for older people."

Funding shortages were identified as the most significant obstacle to the provision of good quality care in community, home and social settings. In particular, reference was made to the lack of resources for home-based services (such as meals-on-wheels) and the lack of supports for family carers. Recent cutbacks in regard to the home-help service were also criticised, with one submission arguing that this service should be put on a legislative base:

"In the absence of a legal obligation to provide [the Home Help Service], it is vulnerable to under-funding, budgetary constraints, and lack of investment in training and the simple infrastructure needed to develop it further ... The Home Help service has to compete for a share of the health budget against service providers who are guaranteed funding because their service is legally mandated. There should be a clear mandatory responsibility for the provision of a Home Help service, based on a detailed needs assessment, and included in an integrated care package which supports the elderly person remaining in their home."

Nursing home care

While nursing homes were generally recognised as an important feature of care for older people, many submissions were critical of them. In particular, concern was expressed about the inadequacy of the regulations underpinning nursing home provision and the lack of formalised review procedures. It was also felt that an insufficient number of nursing homes provide flexible schedules, support independence, and encourage participation in recreational activities. One of the most significant concerns was the lack of facilities within nursing homes to meet the differing needs of low- and high-dependency clients. According to one submission, for example:

"Regrettably, while other countries possess distinct categorisations of long-stay care which care for residents of each specific dependency level, in this country it is typical to find a wide range of older adults, varying in their abilities and afflictions, in a single facility. Given that the nature of the environment is likely to be dictated by the nature of the largest group of residents, which normally constitutes the most dependent individuals, healthier older adults may suffer."

Another concern was the lack of official nursing home inspections, although a number of submissions welcomed the recent announce-ment by the Minister for Health and Children to extend the powers of the Social Services Inspectorate to include residential services for older people and people with disabilities. It was noted that:

"An unacceptable situation precedes this announcement where public nursing homes were not subject to inspections."

Coordination and information

There was considerable comment on the lack of co-ordination of services for older people and lack of information on the level and type of services that are available. A number of barriers to information were highlighted, such as the growing reliance on the Internet. According to one submission:

" ... it is becoming increasingly difficult for [older people] to access relevant information especially if they are not computer literate. Even popular radio shows now refer their listeners to web sites ... We

would like to see a dedicated nationwide IT training programme delivered at times and locations suitable for older people."

An information deficit was also noted in regard to older people's rights and entitlements, with many submissions noting that older people are unaware of the types of services, provisions and funding supports that are available to them.

Training and evaluation

Current services and facilities were also thought to be affected by what were described as 'ageist and dismissive attitudes' from various professionals. One submission put it as follows:

"There is also a sense that their health conditions and treatments are not being adequately explained to them due to assumptions which underrate older peoples' intellectual ability and health awareness."

These types of experiences were largely attributed to a lack of appropriate staff training and service evaluation.

Funding

Problems relating to the inadequacy of funding for services were highlighted throughout the submissions. Serious questions were raised about regulations underpinning various funding mechanisms. It was noted, for example, that some funding streams exclude people aged over 65 years. For example:

"Funding of services provided by the Irish Wheelchair Association is primarily through the physical and sensory budgets at the Health Board Level. However, Government policy underlying these budgets limits the intake of new applicants into services to 0-65 year olds only ... Assessment should determine [a] person's need, not their age."

Submissions also highlighted the difficulties older people face in accessing the Community Support for Older People Grant and many expressed concern about its application process. In particular, it was considered inappropriate that older people must apply for this grant through a relevant community or voluntary group, instead of being able to make an application themselves.

Suggested improvements

Many submissions put forward a range of recommendations for improving existing services and facilities for older people. In general terms, the submissions stressed the need for a comprehensive review of existing services and facilities for older people and a commitment from Government to addressing gaps in provision and to providing a more comprehensive and higher standard of care at all levels. Submissions stressed the importance of involving older people and the organisations that represent them in this process, noting that they are best placed to highlight the changes required. Specific recommendations relating to different aspects of care for older people came under a similar range of headings to those set out in the previous section. These were as follows:

Cost, availability and quality of services

Following on from previous points about the high costs associated with care for older people, submissions drew attention to a range of cost reduction measures. Many of these measures related to reducing the cost of services and facilities for older people themselves. Submissions called on Government to reduce medical care costs for older people by extending medical card provision to all those in receipt of pensions. The removal of waste collection charges was also suggested by a number of submissions and there was a call to make aids and appliances freely available to older people who are in need of them. Some submissions requested that means-testing for alarms, locks and general security be removed, stating that these should be made available to older people as a right. The maintenance and expansion of the Rural Social Transport Scheme was also emphasised. Further cost-reduction strategies for improving the quality of life of older people included expanding the number of home renovation grants available, making reasonably priced retirement homes more readily available, and increasing the level of funding available for the provision of day care centres in areas which do not have them. Others stressed that the cost

of developing more appropriate care could be off-set by saving in other parts of the health services budget, for example:

"Given that many palliative care patients are currently being cared for in inappropriate care settings, the actual additional costs of staff and beds will be largely offset by savings in other areas of the health services."

In terms of the availability of services, submissions stressed the need for more sheltered housing, more respite care, and more day care and social centres. One submission focused almost exclusively on the role of voluntary housing provision in supporting older people who are no longer able to remain living in their own homes. This organisation called for the development and expansion of the voluntary housing sector and in this context, the improved availability of low-support and sheltered housing. Specifically, it noted that:

"Government should adopt a strategy framework for housing and care of the elderly ... Sheltered housing should be available as a first choice alternative to older people no longer able to remain at home."

It added to this recommendation that Government should address constraints in the system which are inhibiting voluntary housing projects by introducing a ring-fenced scheme of revenue funding for care and support costs, increasing the capital funding budget under the Capital Assistance Scheme to bring it in line with NDP targets, improving the limits and budgets for communal facilities in such projects, enhancing the levels of co-ordination between local authorities and health boards and establishing clearer guidelines for funding applications.

A high level of priority was attached to providing a more flexible range of services and to ensuring that these services are available seven days a week and during bank holiday periods. Many submissions stressed the need to expand the meals-on-wheels service and other measures intended to ensure that older people have access to a hot meal. The provision of a meals service during bank holiday and Christmas periods was strongly emphasised. Affordable laundry services for older people was also considered to be necessary, as was a more readily accessible home-help service. Further recommendations for improving the availability of services for older people included providing medical care centres in all rural areas, enhancing the availability of physiotherapy services, providing a dedicated social work service for older people, introducing a rapid response service for crisis intervention, providing breast checks for all older people nationwide, and providing around the clock support for high dependency older people and their carers. Better information on the type of services available was also considered to be a priority, with one submission suggesting the following:

"Easy to read, older people friendly booklet available to all over 60's of every service and facility that is available to them in their areas, with all relevant names and contact phone numbers, that are freephone numbers."

Addressing problems related to the cost and availability of services and facilities was considered to be central to improving the overall quality of care for older people. Further measures for enhancing the quality of care included developing individual care plans and comprehensive home support packages for older people who wish to remain at home, providing higher levels of support for volunteers working with older people, increasing the numbers of dedicated social workers for older people, and developing appropriate capacity-building strategies for carers. In relation to individual care plans, for example, one submission noted that:

"A single assessment process in relation to care management could minimize duplication by the various professionals and service providers. The nursing profession is well placed for the adoption of the role of case manager, as nurses are often the first point of contact with regard to health and social services for the older person."

Another submission stressed that a comprehensive assessment of need should be carried out before an older person is discharged from hospital or when an older person applies for a community care service.

One other recommendation for improving the quality of care was the establishment of a Regulatory Authority to ensure that services are properly registered and to facilitate regular service inspections.

Access to services

Following on from previous points made about the lack of access to transport for many older people, some submissions stressed that free travel should be introduced for all older people. Addressing transport gaps in rural areas and expanding public transport facilities to take in isolated routes were both strongly recommended. Door-to-door pick-up services were also considered necessary in some areas and it was considered important that older people could use their bus passes at any time of the day.

A number of submissions attached a high degree of priority to enhancing the level of funding available for transportation, for example:

"Transportation must be funded to assist the travel of the older person to day care centres, social and shopping trips. Indeed there would be merit in the collaboration between the Health Services and Iarnrod Éireann to work in partnership to provide transport, even at a minimal cost to older people."

Similarly, a considerable number of submissions noted the importance of ensuring that the type of transportation provided is suitable to meet the needs of older people. On this issue, one submission stated:

"A proper transport service with adequate hydraulic lifts for wheelchairs and for people who have difficulty climbing steps for access is essential."

Access to services was also considered to be compromised by geographical variations in the provision of services and submissions noted the importance of addressing these gaps. In relation to community support services, for example, one submission concluded that:

"Comprehensive community support services [should be] available to older people in all parts of Ireland irrespective of geographical location. [There should be] clearly defined and transparent criteria for access to these services and a statutory requirement to provide same."

Primary care and hospital care

In general, it was felt that G.P.s and public health nurses should be more accessible to older people and where necessary, should visit older people in their homes. A number of submissions also stressed the importance of there being a nurse on call around the clock to respond to emergencies. In terms of hospital care, many submissions emphasised the importance of ensuring better quality of care for older people attending hospitals as outpatients. In particular, it was considered that the system of appointments at outpatient's clinics should be reviewed to ensure that older people do not have to wait for care. A similar review was recommended in regard to admissions to hospitals through accident and emergency departments. According to one submission, for example:

"Prompt and easy access to hospital services is essential – a well developed admission and discharge protocol is required to prevent unnecessary delays in returning home."

Other suggestions related to improving ambulance response times in rural areas and ensuring that older people are not discharged from hospitals before adequate follow-up supports have been put in place.

Community, home and social care

The majority of submissions emphasised the

importance of the role played by the community in caring for older people and stressed the need for Government to support work in this area. According to a number of submissions, care for older people should be based on a social rather than a medical model of care. One organisation put it as follows:

"We submit that the approach to provision of services for the elderly should be based on a social care model, which would include medical and nursing needs, rather than on a medical model which patientises the entire group."

Top of the list of recommendations for this area was the expansion and development of the home-help service. Many individuals/organisations emphasised the need to ensure that a high standard of home-help support is provided across the country, for example:

"A home-help service that is of the same standard in all areas. This should be expanded and developed to include homecare service and be more flexible to the changing needs of clients."

It was further felt that the provision of the home-help service should be extended to include evening times and weekends, with much criticism levelled at recent cutbacks in this type of service provision. One submission stressed the need for a home-help service that is managed separately from the public health nurse service and is integrated with the home subvention scheme. The need for increased funding to support home-help was also noted in the majority of the submissions received and it was considered essential that home-help providers are adequately trained and supported to meet the comprehensive needs of the older people they support.

A high level of priority was attached to day care centres and it was suggested that the locations of existing centres should be reviewed to ensure that a sufficient number of them are in place throughout the country. Much attention was also given to the contribution made by the meals-on-wheels service, with one submission noting the following:

"At present there is no standardisation of meals provision for the elderly, largely because this service is discretionary. Meals provision is dependent on partnerships between voluntary groups and the health board, and often these arrangements are ad hoc and dependent on individual goodwill of Health Board personnel and volunteers. A framework needs to be drawn up which ensures an effective interface between voluntary agencies and the statutory sector, ensuring consistency, continuity and transparency of service provision."

A key concern for many groups was that the meals-on-wheels service be extended to rural areas and again, that it be available at times suitable to older people.

Widespread support was expressed across the submissions for a range of voluntary and community support structures to meet the needs of older people. One submission put it as follows:

"There is an absolute need to develop initiatives to involve and include older people in their community, to liaise with voluntary and community support structures in order to facilitate inclusion of the older citizen thus avoiding isolation and loneliness ..."

In essence, it was felt that older people should have a choice of services available to them in order to support them to continue living at home, should they wish to do so. Thus, as well as enhancing day centres, social centres, home-help services and meals-on-wheels, submissions stressed the need for night carers, home security, public health nurses, and emergency response units. Attention was also given to the need to put additional supports in place for older people with special needs, for example:

" ... appropriate measures are needed in order to ensure that services can respond to older people with disabilities, so that realistic expectations can be set and that they can live in the community."

Nursing home care

In response to the criticisms levelled at nursing homes, submissions emphasised the need to ensure that there is a high standard of care across all nursing homes in the country. A number of submissions recommended putting in place legislation to ensure that nursing homes include an appropriate nurse/client ratio. Further recommendations related to the accreditation of nursing home provision, with one submission in particular providing an accurate summary of the sentiments expressed across many of the submissions received:

"Agencies that accredit nursing homes need to incorporate indicators that address safety and quality of life issues in their assessment. A social, psychological and medical review with the option for discharge planning is needed in nursing homes. Policies to increase the numbers of Registered Nurses in nursing homes to a level considered adequate by professional standards should be the goals. Training and evaluation for support staff is also necessary."

A small number of submissions also suggested that a Recreational Therapist be included in all nursing homes with a view to undertaking individual assessments of the quality of life needs of each resident and ensuring that these needs are met.

Coordination and information

A strong recommendation across the submissions was that voluntary and community organisations and State agencies should work together in partnership to deliver care for older people. A clear call was made for better integration of health and personal social services and provisions in the Health Act 2004 requiring the Health Services Executive to integrate the delivery of these services were particularly welcomed. One submission put it as follows:

"Citizen Information Centres frequently report cases of people coming home from hospital without arrangements being made for the services they need to enable them to fully recover at home and to support their living at home. Integration of services

does not only mean that the hospital authorities should inform the community care services that a person is being discharged. This assessment should be carried out while the person is in hospital or while attending a day hospital service."

It was also felt that housing policy should be co-ordinated with policies on health and social services with one submission noting that while local authorities and health authorities provide assistance with housing repairs, "neither provides help as of right and adequate resources are not provided for these services."

Further recommendations related to ensuring that older people are aware of their rights and entitlements. The idea of a one-stop-shop was proposed to support older people's access to relevant information and to assist them to make informed choices. One submission felt that this should be a mobile one-stop-shop, delivering information directly to people's homes.

The production of user-friendly information booklets on the services and facilities available to older people was proposed and it was suggested that day care and social centres, nursing homes, hospitals, nurses and G.P.'s could all play a stronger role in disseminating this type of information.

Poor levels of information relating to the absence of an independent complaints and appeals system within the health services were also noted, with a number of submissions requesting that the Health Services Executive put such a system in place as soon as possible.

Training and evaluation

The need for ongoing training for health and social care staff was recommended in a considerable number of the submissions. This, it was felt, is essential to ensure that services are appropriately sensitive and responsive to older people's needs. One submission recommended the following:

"We recommend that all training of health professionals incorporates age-awareness and that an advocacy service for older people, particularly those in residential care should be established."

Submissions also strongly supported the need for services to be evaluated on an ongoing basis and suggested that appropriate regulations be introduced to ensure that services respond to the recommendations arising from these evaluations.

Funding

It was noted that " ... all services seem to be operating on a shoe string." Based on this, submissions called for Government to make more funding available for home help, day centres, meals-on-wheels and respite care. More funding was also recommended to both train and pay social care staff.

It was noted that the allocation of funding from different Government Departments can be confusing and based on this, a small number of submissions recommended making funding available through a single department, for example:

"All care should be funded from one source rather than be spread between different funds across departments. One of the strangest experiences for families with a member in need of care is the contrast between the difficulty with which they qualify for small financial and other supports when care is provided within the family and part-funded via the Social Welfare budget, and the ease with which they access much greater funds via the Health department's nursing subvention scheme. Were caring costs derived from the same fund, government oversight would be improved in terms of supporting choice and making cost benefit analyses."

Supporting older people to live at home

The stated objective of public policy with respect to the long-term care of older people, i.e. to assist them to remain in their own homes for as long as possible, was welcomed in the vast majority of submissions received. However, a number of submissions noted that the Government's policy of supporting home-based care is not followed through in practice. In this context, much attention was drawn to differences in provision for institutional care and home-based care, for example:

"At present there is a legal entitlement to nursing home subventions. There is no corresponding legal right to care in one's own home. This skews the balance in favour of nursing home care over care in one's home which would be most people's first choice ... While the stated policy of successive governments has been in favour of home-based care, the reality is that institutional care of the elderly has tended to crowd out the development of adequate home-care supports."

On this same point, another submission noted the following:

"The policy of promoting care at home requires that the supports available for home living are at least as great as those available for institutional living. This is not always the case. For example, an older person who qualifies for a private nursing home subvention should be able to avail of that subvention in order to live at home. The tax relief that is available to the person who pays the nursing home fees should also be available if the nursing care or other domestic care is contracted at home."

Reference was made to the Mercer proposals on 'financing long-term care' (2002) which recommended that recipients of care be given a choice between receiving services in kind or a cash amount to pay for privately-sourced care, with one submission noting that "the thrust of the report is a rebalancing of state assistance with care costs towards care in the community rather than the current emphasis on institutional care."

Submissions identified a range of additional supports as being necessary to supporting older people who wish to remain living at home. These were as follows:

Health-based supports

It was felt that older people living at home require more and better access to primary care and hospital care. It was noted, however, that variations in healthcare provision across the country present real obstacles for some older people wishing to remain at home. A specific concern was the lack of specialist health services in certain areas, particularly for older people with high dependencies on such care. Another key consideration was the limited availability of public health nurses and home-help services. In relation to the nursing home subvention scheme, one submission suggested the following:

"There should be a choice given to the older person/their carers, to use the "nursing home" subvention fee to purchase nursing and ancillary care in their own homes instead of going into a nursing home. This would have the great benefit of maintaining the older person in their home for a longer period."

Another submission recommended the introduction of nurse-led units into all community care areas with the primary function of facilitating the services required to maintain healthy older people in their homes.

Family and community-based supports

A strong emphasis was placed on the need to support family members who have responsibility for caring for older people. In this context, submissions highlighted the importance of ensuring that respite care is readily available to those who require it and that family members can avail of wider supports from within the community. Support was also expressed for a model of homecare assistance that:

" ... gives care recipients a choice between receiving services in kind or a (lower) cash amount to pay for privately-sourced care or give recognition to family members providing care."

Community-based services were emphasised as being particularly important to older people wishing to remain at home. Particular attention was drawn to the role played by day care centres in promoting positive mental health and in providing an opportunity to socialise. Other important community-based supports for older people living at home were identified as meals-on-wheels services, laundry services, and shopping services.

Housing supports

A range of housing supports was identified as being critical to older people wishing to remain at home. It was noted that although home ownership is high among older people in Ireland, older people experience higher levels of housing deprivation than other members of society. Reference was made to the social and sheltered housing plans set in the 1998 Housing Act and concern was expressed that the houses built under this plan do not meet the special needs required for older people. It was considered essential that older people's houses are adapted to meet their particular needs, with downstairs bathrooms and bedrooms installed, where necessary. The major delays experienced by older people in being assessed for the Disabled Person's Grant was noted in a number of submissions, with many more stressing the need for appropriate provisions to be put in place to assist older people to upgrade their homes to the standards required. Adequate heating was identified as a priority issue and was often referred to in the context of improving home insulation. It was also considered important that appropriate sheltered accommodation be provided, especially for older people who do not have family members and who wish to remain living in their own communities.

Personal and financial supports

A key consideration for older people wishing to remain at home is security. Many submissions referred to the importance of older people having safety locks on their doors, outside security lights, fire alarms, mobile phones, and panic buttons. It was felt that these safety measures should be provided to all older people as a right and, as stated above, dissatisfaction was expressed with the current grant scheme of providing personal alarms and other security equipment to older people. The provision of regular surveillance visits of older people's homes and the development of a uniform countywide system for use of personal alarms by older people were suggested as security measures. A welcome development was identified as the introduction of pendants for safety and security.

It was noted that there are limited financial supports available to older people to obtain the type of provisions necessary to secure their homes. In this context, many submissions argued for increased pension provision and to improve the eligibility criteria for accessing grants and provisions.

Other supports

Lack of transportation in certain areas was identified as a seriously debilitating factor for older people wishing to remain at home. For this reason, submissions advocated the need for an expanded public transportation system and the provision of subsidised or free transport to support older people in accessing hospital care, respite care, day care and other services.

The design of homes and the accessibility of the built environment were identified as having an important role to play in supporting the physical independence of older people and it was noted that many houses and public buildings were built prior to the accessibility requirements in the existing planning/building control codes. A number of submissions endorsed the principle of universal design, with one submission welcoming the provision in the 2006 budget for *"an allocation to local authorities to address accessibility issues in public buildings and streets."*

More accessible information on older people's rights and entitlements was also prioritised for older people wishing to remain at home. It was felt that older people and their families are often unaware of the type of health-, community- and home-based supports and provisions that are available to them and it was stressed that this issue should be addressed as a priority.

Conclusion

Delivering appropriate changes in each of the areas set out above was considered to be critical to improving the current system of care for older people in Ireland. In summing up, one submission said the following:

"... when older people are asked their preferences in terms of care, they express a preference for care in their own homes. In our experience, the provision of adequate community care services continues to be patchy and somewhat ad hoc and its unavailability can lead to hardship for large numbers of people. There needs to be an adequate system of care for older people and existing government policy on the provision of services to older people, as set out in reports like 'The Years Ahead', and 'Quality and Fairness', needs to be implemented."

A small number of submissions noted that there should be a Minister of State for Older People and that this Minister should be based in the Department of Health and Children. The Government, in particular the Department of Health and Children, was identified as having primary responsibility for delivering the suggested improvements to existing services and provision, although many submissions concluded that changes in this area should be based on close collaboration with the Health Services Executive, local authorities, local service providers, community and voluntary organisations, and older people themselves.

List of submissions received

Active Retirement Group, Cahirciveen

Active Retirement Group, Tarbert

Acute and Community,
Health Service Executive, Southern Area

Abbey Health Care Ltd (x2)

Age Action Ireland Ltd (North Dublin)

Age & Opportunity

Alzheimer Day Care Centre, Boherbee, Tralee

Ardfert Carers Group, Co. Kerry

Ardfert Community Council Ltd

Area Development Management Ltd

Baile Mhuire Recreation and Respite Centre

Ballinskelligs Community Care

Ballyduff Active Retirement Group

Ballylongford ICA and Active Retirement

Ballymacelliott Active Retirement Association

Ballyroan Community Care Group

Beaufort Community Care Group, Killarney

Blerrerville Active Retired Association

Bonane Community Council

Bray Partnership

Cahirciveen Social Services

CARE Local, Dublin

Care of Elderly Units, Kerry General Hospital

Carers Services Office,
Health Service Executive, Southern Region

Margaret Casey, ICA and Women's Network

Castlecomer District Community Development Network

Castlegregory Care of the Aged

Castleisland Active Retirement Group

Castleisland Community Centre (x5)

Castlemaine Community Care

Causeway Social Care Group

Choice Project,
Health Service Executive North West Region

Club Ide Active Retirement Association

Comhairle

Community Occupational Therapy,
Health Service Executive, Dublin South

Conference of Religious in Ireland

City District

Mr Noel Collins

Community Services Area 6 (Dublin)

Community Services, Clondalkin

Community Services,
Health Service Executive, Southern Region

Community Work Department, Kerry Community
Services, Health Service Executive, Southern Region

Continuing Care Unit, Coolnagarrane, Skibbereen,
Health Service Executive, Southern Region

Conference of Religious of Ireland (CORI)

Council for Services to Older People,
North West Inner City Dublin

Cross Border Development, Older People's Project

Dr Nell Crushell, Senior Area Medical Officer,
Health Service Executive Southern Region

Cúin Dídin Residential Care

Cunamh Energy Action Ltd

Cumann Cabhrach na Sean, Killarney

Currow/Curran Parish Council

Ms Mary Daly

Disability Federation of Ireland

Mr Kieran Doyle

Dromid-Waterville Community Care Group

Duagh Family Resource Centre Ltd.

Economic and Social Research Institute

Emergency Response

11-One Club Shanakill

Firies/Ballyhar Community Care

Fochoiste na Seanoirí,
Comhar Chumann Dhún Chaoin Teo

Fold TeleCare

Garda Siochana, Chief Superintendent's Office,
Eastern Division

Gerontological Nursing Development Group,
Cork Kerry Region

Glenveigh/Chomane Community Council

Ms Louise Halloran

Anne Harris, Home Help Organiser

Health Promotion Department,
Health Services Executive, Southern Area

Henderson Foley Management Consultants

Ms Kathleen Herlihy, Co-ordinator of Home Care
Services (Alzheimer), North Kerry

Holy Cross Day Care Centre, Killarney (x2)

Irish Council for Social Housing

Irish Hospice Foundation

Irish Human Rights Commission

Inch Community Council

Irish Nurses Organisation

Irish Pharmaceutical Union

Irish Senior Citizens Parliament

Irish Wheelchair Association

Kenmare Community Hospital

Kerry Mental Health Services

Kerry Community Services, Care Group for Older People,
Health Services Executive

Mr Denis Kidney, St Joseph's Nursing Home

Kilcummin Community Care

Kilgarvan Community Care

Killarney Active Retirement

Ms Helen Killiride

Laundry for the Elderly, Listowel

Mr Robert Lee

Listry Community Council

Mature Ladies Group, Kerins O'Rahilly's GAA Club

Mfg-Meitheal Mhúscraí & Comhlucht Tithe
an tSulán Teo

Ms Yvonne Maher

Ms Linda McKernon

Mr Vince Moore

Multi Disciplinary Sector Team, Health Service
Executive, Southern Region

Muintir na Tíre Community Alert Programme

National Council for the Blind, Cuman Iosaef Teo

National Disability Authority

Nursing Midwifery Planning and Development Unit,
Health Service Executive Eastern Region

Older Women's Network (Ireland)

Patrons of Killorglin Day Care Centre, Co. Kerry (x9)

Patrons of St Patrick's Day Care Centre, Co. Kerry (x5)

Physiotherapy Staff in Co. Kerry

Ms Ber Power,
Continuing Care Placement Co-ordinator, Killarney

Practice Development Nurses, HSE Western Region

Rehab Group

Ms Geraldine Rigney, Care Group Co-ordinator

Ms Kathy Sinnott, MEP

South Kerry Older People's Network

South West Kerry Women's Association

Sneem Welfare Company

Spa/Fenit ICA

St Brigid's Community Centre, Tralee

St Bridget's Senior Citizens Group, Galway (x2)

St Columbanus Home, Health Service Executive,
Southern Region

St Vincent de Paul, Castleisland

St Vincent de Paul Day Care Centre, Lixnaw, Co. Kerry

St Vincent De Paul Society, Listowel

Third Age Centre, Summerhill Active Retirement Group

Tralee '97 Probus Club

Tralee Womens Resource Centre

Ms Patricia Treacy, Public Health Nurse

Tuosist Community Care

Dr Kieran Walsh, University of Limerick

Women's Health Council

West Kerry Care of the Aged Company Ltd (x2)

WISE

Annex 4   Care for Older People: International Developments

The countries reviewed in this section, the UK, Australia, Canada, Denmark, Finland, France, the Netherlands, Sweden and New Zealand, all have an ageing population profile. Each country predicts that there will be a significant increase in the population of those over the age of 65 years in the next two decades. Many countries, for example Australia, Finland and France, expect the numbers to double in the next 40 years. Table A4.1 below gives an overall picture of the numbers of those over the age of 65 years in each country and the percentages of those in institutional care and of those who receive homecare.

These countries were chosen for comparative reasons as they all are highly developed and they have significantly increasing ageing populations. They also have produced innovative policies, which could prove useful in informing future policies in regard to care for older people in this country.

The most predominant trend to emerge is that all these countries recognise the importance of maintaining an older person's independence and so encourage them to remain living in their own home for as long as possible. Over the last two decades most of these countries have pursued a policy of de-institutionalisation, where the focus has been on preventing older

Table A4.1 Breakdown of Total Population, Population of Those Over the Age of 65 Years and % of Those in Institutional Care and of Those Who Receive Homecare, for Each Country

	Total Population (2004)	Population over 65+ (2004)	% of those over 65+ in institutional care (2000)	% of those over 65+ who receive home-care (2000)
UK	59,600,000	11,014,000	5.1% (2002)	20.3% (2002)
Australia	20,225,925	2,370,878	6.8%	11.7%
Canada	31,946,300	4,141,000	7.5%	15%
Denmark	5,360,000	791,000 (2000)	3.3%	23%
Finland	5,219,732	813,195	7.6%	14%
France	60,424,213	9,891,039	6.5%	6.1%
Netherlands	16,258,032	2,230,000	8.8%	12%
Sweden	8,875,053	1,533,609	8.7%	11.2%
New Zealand	4,095,068	450,426	8.7%	11.2%

people, even those who require a high level of care, from entering into institutional care. These countries have tried to provide alternatives to institutional care, namely, developing health and social services, to be delivered to the older person in their own home. However, some countries, for example Sweden and Denmark provide more comprehensive homecare services than other countries, for example France and Canada. While countries, like France and Canada recognise the importance of allowing the older person to remain living independently, their homecare services are underdeveloped, particularly in Canada. While in France, policy is focused equally on both institutional care and home care services for older people.

There has been a move, in many of these countries, over the last 10 years towards allowing more individual choice for older people in regard to the type of homecare services they receive. For example, consumer-directed care programmes have been introduced in countries like France and the Netherlands. This type of programme allows the person in need of care to choose and design their own homecare package, which they feel would best suit their own needs. The programme is intended to empower the older person to choose and manage their own care.

More recently, there has been a shift in focus towards informal carers (care provided by family and friends). Initially most homecare services were directed away from family carers. However, it has been found that many homecare schemes aiming to allow older people in need of care to remain living in their own homes are in fact heavily dependent on informal carers. This has led to a policy re-think in many countries, on the role of the informal carer and it has led to the belief that services should be provided to informal carers looking after older people rather than entirely directing the services towards older people themselves. A number of measures taken include:

In the UK, carers have now been given a statutory right to receive an assessment of need for services, in addition to services for older people.

Some countries have introduced respite-care services to provide carers with a break from caring responsibilities; for example in Finland, carers are entitled to two free days a month during a period of time that the nature of care they are providing is very demanding. During this statutory free time, the local authority is responsible for providing care to the older recipient. In Australia, the government has quadrupled expenditure on respite care. However, in other countries, the potential demand for respite care remains considerably higher than provision, for example in Canada, potential demand for respite care is around four times higher than the current use of the service (OECD, 2005).

Several countries, like Canada, Sweden, the UK and Finland, all have introduced payments to carers to compensate for employment income lost due to caring.

It has been recognised that good co-ordination of multi-disciplinary care (health, social services, informal care) is vital for people receiving care at home, to ensure that all their needs are catered for. However, there have been problems in the co-ordination of these services in many countries. One concept developed to overcome these problems is to measure how successfully different health and social services fit together, this is called the 'continuum of care'. The main policy aim behind the continuum of care approach is to have services managed in such a way as to achieve a more co-ordinated input of a range of services required by service users and families at any one point in time, and to have better management of transitions between service and service settings as the patient's needs change and develop over time.

Certain countries have introduced measures to improve the linkages between agencies providing health and social services to older people, by developing strategic frameworks. Both the UK (National Service Framework for Older People) and New Zealand (Positive Ageing Strategy) have published strategic frameworks. There are examples of countries also, that have introduced measures to improve the integration of services, for example, Australia employs Aged Care Assessment Teams (ACATs) to carry out multi-disciplinary assessment of those in need of care. In Denmark, problems in the co-ordination of services were overcome by merging home-care services with domiciliary health care, so that conflicts that emerged, previously between health and social care staff, could be avoided.

Each of these countries is faced with the challenge to provide good quality and compre-hensive health and social care services to increasing numbers of older people. Each country too, in its own right has developed policies in care for older people, which they feel would best serve its own ageing people. However, the overarching policy to emerge from all the countries reviewed is that services should be provided to enable older people to remain living independently and avoid institutionalisation for as long as possible.

The following section details current and innovative policies developed for each of the selected countries.

The United Kingdom

Current Policy

UK policy on care for older people acknowledges the role family/friends/relatives play and that much of the care given to older people is provided by them. Current policy recognises and encourages this informal care, by providing a cash benefit to informal carers called the Carer's Allowance. To be eligible, carers must have limited employment income and be providing a minimum of 35 hours a week to a person who is themselves in receipt of a benefit awarded to those dependent on others. Until 2002, the Carer's Allowance was only awarded to carers aged below 65 years, but eligibility has since been extended beyond this age[10].

There is also a strong policy emphasis on recognising the role of the user and taking into account the views and opinions of the older person when developing future policy and services for older people.

In terms of provision, care for older people comprises a range of health and social care services delivered locally by National Health Service (NHS) bodies and local councils with social work responsibilities.

In the UK, long-term care is provided in residential or nursing homes for older people. This care is either provided by the NHS or by the local authorities and social services, depending on what type of care is required. For example, if more medical care is needed, then the NHS provides the care in hospitals or long-term care institutions and if more welfare care is needed, the local authorities provide this type of care in residential homes. Residential homes range from very basic where older people have their own rooms, share facilities such as laundry services and have their meals cooked for them, to homes which provide specialist care and supervision 24 hours a day. Long term-care can also be provided by private organisations, where the residents are expected to cover the entire cost themselves.

There is also retirement accommodation available to older people in the UK. These are housing set-ups where there is a resident warden or caretaker who can be summoned by an emergency alarm if needed. People in these retirement homes usually share facilities like laundry services, sitting rooms, gardens and various professionals like hairdressers or chiropodists[11].

Homecare in the form of domiciliary services is provided to those in need of assistance and care in their own homes, by the local authorities and social services.

---

10. OECD (2005) 'Long-term care policies for older people'

11. 'Going into Care' –
    http://www.bbc.co.uk/health/health_over/50/practialities_care.shtlm.

Access to care is usually determined by certain levels of eligibility. The funding of care is partly provided from the public sector through taxation and partly provided by private means.

Innovative Policies

The *National Service Framework for Older People* was published in the UK in 2001, to look at the problems older people face in receiving care in order to deliver higher quality services. This Framework set out eight standards which aim to provide person-centred care, remove age discrimination, promote older people's health and independence and to fit services around people's needs. The eight standards set out by the Framework were:

— to eradicate age discrimination in the health and social care services;

— to support person-centred care with newly integrated services;

— to provide intermediate care services to older people at home or in designated care settings;

— to make sure that general hospital care for older people is delivered through appropriate specialist care and by staff that have the right skills to meet their needs;

— to ensure that the health care services take action to prevent strokes, working in partnership with other agencies where appropriate;

— to take action to prevent falls and reduce resultant fractures or other injuries to older people;

— to ensure that older people with mental health problems have access to integrated mental health services, provided by both the health and social care services; and

— to promote the health and well-being of the older person through a co-ordinated programme of action led by the NHS and supported by the local authorities[12].

In 2003, the Department of Health in the UK published a progress report on the *National Service Framework for Older People,* which details the progress the Department of Health has made since the start of the Framework. It has made a number of advancements in the area of general well-being of older people; for example, the number of operations performed on older people over 65 years has increased since 2001; Single Assessment Process (SAP) was introduced to ensure that older people get a good quality of integrated care, but only have to be assessed once through a multi-disciplinary, inter-agency body so it cuts down on red tape and saves the older person from having to apply to a range of different agencies. The report also highlighted that the number of people receiving intensive care in their own home has also increased from 72,300 to 77,400 between 2001 and 2002; the length of hospital stays for stroke patients has been shortened and there has been a significant increase in the number of stroke physicians employed in UK hospitals also. In addition, there have been a number of programmes launched in the UK that promote healthy and active lives for older people, for example, in Blackburn they have launched the 'Up for Owt' programme which organises a range of physical activities for older people in that area[13].

Over the years, there have been communication problems and disputes between the health and social services in regard to the co-ordinating services for older people. To overcome these problems, the UK Government, since 1997, has actively promoted improved integration between health and social services. As a result of this, Care Trusts have been established. These Care Trusts are fully single, multi-purpose legal bodies to commission and be responsible for the delivery of all local health and social care to older people and other groups. They are seen as an appropriate response to the problems often experienced by many older people when they

---

12. *National Service Framework for Older People –*
   http://www.dh.gov.uk/PublicationsAndStatistics/Publications/PublicationsPolicy
   AndGuidance/PublicationsPolicyAndGuidanceArticle/fs/en?CONTENT_ID=40030
   66&chk=wg3bgo .

13. *Department of Health (2003) 'National Service Framework for Older People: A*
   Report of Progress and Future Challenges.

are released from hospital care and are in need of further support. However, Care Trusts have not proved to be popular and only eight of them have been set up in the UK so far. Reasons cited for the low take-up include: the establishing of Care Trusts is too expensive for many authorities and instead they have looked to alternative, less expensive models to integrate services; many feel it takes too much time to set them up due to the organisational change that has to take place in setting up these Trusts; there have also been problems in combining health and social services as many health and social services staff are suspicious of each other and also some social services staff fear that health care will dominate in the new Care Trusts. Nevertheless, some people feel that existing Care Trusts are a platform for success[14].

In 2002, the Audit Commission's report *Integrated Services for Older People* recommended that services must work together to adequately meet the needs of older people. In response to this a 'whole system' approach has been taken in delivering services to older people. This approach places the older person in the centre, involves the older person as a partner, who has a voice on how services are shaped and delivered. It has been advised by the Audit Commission that many agencies, which work with older people, including many non-specialist services, such as transport, education and housing, as well as services that provide care should come together to deliver care to the older people in an integrated and comprehensive way. This 'whole system' approach also encourages the better management of the care system as whole.

In regard to funding of long-term care in the UK, the *Royal Commission Report on long-term Care of the older people (1999)* recommended that the State should improve funding provision. It recommended that the costs of care for those

individuals who need it should be split between living costs, housing costs and personal care. The Commission advised that personal care should be available after an assessment, according to need and paid for from a general taxation; the rest should be subject to a co-payment according to means. However, it ought to be noted that while Scotland has introduced free personal care, England, Wales and Northern Ireland have introduced free nursing care in nursing homes but have not introduced free personal care.

Australia

Current Policy

Australia provides long-stay care in institutions and community care is provided to older people in their own homes or in residential care facilities, sometimes with help from community services e.g. home-help, district nurses and delivered meals. Over the past few years, there have been a number of reforms made, for example the *Aged Care Act (1997)* brought about reforms which have led to improved arrange-ments for long-stay care and increased provision of community care. However, the *HiT*[15] report highlighted that many people in rural and remote areas, not only suffer from poorer health but also have difficultly in accessing health care services due to the difficulty in recruiting and maintaining health professionals in rural communities. The Aged Care Act reforms have gone some way to improving access to services for older people.

The Australian Government is responsible for funding much of the care for older people. However residents in residential aged care homes may be expected to pay care fees and accommodation payments (which are means-tested); additional services required have to be financed by the residents themselves. Hardship

---

14. *Community Care. 2005. 'Distinct Cooling on Care Trusts revealed in plan for adult services' Community Care Magazine, 31st of March, 2005.*

15. *Health Care Systems in Transition – Australia, WHO Regional Office for Europe on behalf of European Observatory on Health Systems and Policies, 2001.*

allowances are now available to those unable to meet the costs of their stay in residential aged care homes.

Innovative Policies

In 1992, Community Aged Care Packages (CACPS) were introduced as a community-based alternative for people who would otherwise qualify for entry into residential care. These Care Packages are an individually-tailored package of care services for older people in their own homes. These care services are multi-disciplinary and include geriatricians, physicians, registered nurses, social workers, physiotherapists and psychologists. Older people eligible for these packages follow a comprehensive assessment by Aged Care Assessment Teams (ACAT). They assess people using a multi-disciplinary and multi-dimensional approach. Their needs are assessed and it is then determined what services should be provided to them. The ACAT also assesses older people for other types of care packages available, for example access to residential aged care and the Extended Aged Care at Home (EACH). The EACH programme assists frail aged people to remain in their homes, supported by high level care through an approved service provider. These community care packages and the Aged Care Assessment Teams are jointly funded and administered by the Commonwealth government and the states under co-operative working arrangements.

For those who are cared for on an informal basis, the Australian Government funds a number of services to support the informal carer. These services include; the Carer Payment which is an income-support payment for people whose caring responsibilities prevent them from working; the Carer Allowance is an income supplement for people who provide daily care to a relative; the National Respite for Carers Programme, which provides funding for short term or emergency respite in the community. The programme provides information, counselling and support for carers, as well as assistance to help them take a break from caring (OECD, 2005).

Canada

Current Policy

In Canada, care for older people is organised on two levels: institutional care and home-based care. Institutional care is focused on the provision of long-term care and chronic care. These institutions can range from residential care facilities, which provide only limited services, to intensive chronic care facilities, which provide care for high-need patients. Access to long-term care can be available through the traditional health care system or by the individuals themselves; however, for the most part, access to residential institutions is a personal choice.[16]

Canada does not have a universally accessible, comprehensive home-care policy because home-care falls outside the realm of *Medicare*. However, the Canadian government does recognise that homecare for older people is a 'necessary part of an integrated and appropriate health care system'[17]. Various Canadians reports have supported and called for policies to be created to promote and support homecare and that homecare should be recognised as a basis for a comprehensive health care system for all older Canadians. While it has been recognised that more resources should be allocated to community care programmes, Canada is reluctant to do this because of fiscal pressures (Home Care in Canada, 1999).

Long-stay care in Canada is funded by the provincial government, while accommodation costs (room & board) are paid either by the individual or by private social insurance. While there is a lack of information surrounding community care for older people in Canada, it seems that homecare services are funded through provincial government health budgets but since many homecare services fall outside the realm *of Medicare,* there are no standardised arrangements for funding, eligibility and user fees (Home Care in Canada, 1999).

16. 'Heath Care Systems in Transition – Canada' (1996) WHO Regional Office for Europe on behalf of European Observatory on Health Systems and Polices

17. 'Home Care in Canada' (1999) by the Canadian association on Gerontology: policy statement on homecare

Innovative Policies

Home-care in Canada can take many forms from physician visits, specialised nursing care and home-maker services to meal-on-wheels programmes and adult day-care. It has been recognised that home-care services tend to be provided by many different organisations. In response to this, some provinces are now offering one-stop-shopping, by organising these services around one access point.

It has also been recognised that between 70-80% of home-care is provided on an informal basis by family and friends. In response to this, the Canadian Government introduced a new cash benefit scheme to provide short-term support to carers in 2004. This scheme is called *Compassionate Care Benefit (CCB)* and it offers 'Employment Insurance' eligible workers who are absent from work in order to provide care to a close family member who has a serious illness, financial assistance (OECD, 2005). However, while the Canadian government believes that this type care is very important, it also believes that there are limitations attached to informal care, caused by changes in demographic and contemporary society; so the Canadian government believe that there is a need to look to alternative supports in order to meet the needs of older people[18].

Denmark

Current Policy

Denmark's nursing homes supply both residential care and day care services to older people. These homes are run by the municipalities (local governments in Denmark) and are mainly financed by the inhabitants, although for those on low income, the expenses of care are paid using a proportion of their old age pension. Since 1987, nursing homes have been considered ordinary housing, with the rights and duties of nursing homes inhabitants being the same as the rest of the population.

Home-care services are widely available in Denmark. The basic purpose of home-care is to provide assistance with basic housekeeping and personal care. This includes a variety of tasks performed by helpers. There is also a wide variation in the amount of help received by different clients. This ranges from a client receiving help for a few hours every week to a client receiving help for several hours every day. Over the past decade, there has been a large increase in the numbers receiving home-care and a considerable increase in the numbers availing of home-care services for several hours every day. The average number of hours allocated to persons over 67 years is five hours a week. Home-care is provided to those on the basis of need. An assessment is carried out by the municipalities to determine what kind of home-care services the older person needs. Home-care services are provided free of charge to all older people in Denmark[19]. This extensive system of home-help makes it possible for many chronically and terminally ill patients to stay in their own home for as long as possible.

It has recently been acknowledged in Denmark that the increasing number of older people will prove a heavy burden on the municipalities in the future, so they are now looking for ways to reduce the costs. In response to this, health and social authorities are attempting to place more emphasis on self-care, increased support for people to remain in their homes for as long as possible and increased health promotion activity. However, some predict that contracting services out to private non-profit agencies and patient co-payments will become increasingly popular in Denmark in the future as a way of combating the increasing financial burden.

There is no policy in regard to access to care for older people in Denmark, as this country pursues a policy of universality, where benefits and services are available to all, regardless of their income.

---

18. Ross, M. M. 1991. 'Beyond the family: informal support in later life' in PUBMED-online database.

19. 'Home Care in Denmark' (2000) – online source:
   http://www.sfi.dk/graphics/SFI/Pdf/Working_papers/workingpaper2000_12.pdf

Innovative Policies

Denmark is recognised to be well ahead of its European neighbours in regard to pursuing a policy of de-institutionalisation. In 1988, legislation stopped the building of nursing homes and instead encouraged the building of specialised units for older people who would be supported by home-care services, which focuses more on a personal domestic help. These specialised units can be described as a group of 12-20 specialised dwellings, arranged in such a way as to create a small group-type community which has a common service centre, from which both district nurses and home helps operate. The main aim of this type of care is to enable the older person to receive whatever care is required while having the opportunity to remain living independently.

In terms of informal care, Denmark places no legal obligation on the family to provide care. Families are not expected nor obliged to care for an older family member, once they become dependent. Homecare services have long been established to replace informal carers. In fact, 'informal carer' is not part of the Danish policy discourse. The one exception to this is care by spouses, in that the presence of a spouse in the household is taken into account in service allocation and there are still implied obligations on spouses.[20]

Danish care policies have been found to be well resourced (there has been a large increase in the number of home nurses and home helps employed by municipalities) and have proven very popular. This is reflected in the dramatic decrease in the numbers of those in nursing homes in the last 20 years, with the numbers of people in homes falling from 50,000 in 1987 to 36,500 in 1996 (HiT, 2001).

The problems of co-ordination and collaboration between the health and social services in Denmark are less acute than in other countries and this may be because the home-help service

has been merged there with domiciliary health care to overcome conflicts between health and social care staff and because all of these home-care services are the responsibility of municipalities.

Since 1997, municipalities are required to establish locally elected 'elder councils' whose remit is to advise councils on elder policy and issues, and to represent the interests of older users with respect to older people care and service charges.

Finland

Current Policy

Finland has a comprehensive, integrated and multi-disciplinary care structure for its older population. The main types of services available in Finland include institutional care, home-help, home nursing care, housing and transport services.

Institutional care can be given for part of the day, or on a short-term or long-term basis. Statutory institutional care services include institutional services provided in nursing homes, in in-patient wards of regional health centres and in specialised care units.

Short-term institutional care provides care for a short period of time and it also provides respite to family care givers. Usually, periods of short-term institutional care can be regular when they alternate with living at home. The fees for short-term institutional care are generally fixed. The main aim of short-term institutional care is to prevent the need for permanent care in an institution.

Long-term institutional care is provided by various types of nursing homes. NGOs and private firms also provide institutional care in nursing homes and private hospitals. This type of care is provided when round-the-clock care can no longer be provided at home. This care entails full-board, medication, hygiene, clothing and services promoting social well-being. Fees

20. With Respect to Old Age – 'Policy Options for Informal Carers' online source: http://www.archive.official-documents.co.uk/document/cm41/4192/v3p.pdf

for long-term institutional care are determined according to the older person's income; fees can account for up to 80% of their income. Access to this type of care is determined by a regional working group, which includes at least a health visitor or home helper, a doctor responsible for long-term care in the region and a social worker concerned with older people's welfare.

In Finland, the home-help services and nursing care work in close collaboration with each other. Home-help is provided to help with everyday activities. Home nursing services are used by people of all ages, though it is mainly used by the increasing number of older people in Finland and it mainly provides health care to older people. In some regions of Finland, home-help services and home nursing services have been combined to form homecare services (similar to the Danish model).

Home support is also given to older people. This is done by carrying out improvements in the older person's home to suit their needs, for example widening door openings and providing a stair lift.

Finland also provides 'service housing' to those who need support inside and outside the home. These 'service homes' provide both accommodation and services to older people, while enabling them to remain living independently. 'Service housing' can be a block of flats, a group of service homes, or an individual service home, and is arranged by municipalities, special organisations or by private firms. Many nursing homes in Finland have been turned into service housing.

Transport services are offered to any older person who has trouble getting around and who cannot use public transport. This is arranged mainly by taxi, although group transport has become increasingly popular in Finland. Clients pay the same fare as they would for public transport.

The financing of care for older people is considered a public responsibility. Social services including community care are financed by municipal taxes, State subsidies and user charges. However due to tighter fiscal considerations, some of the municipalities in

Finland have shown an interest in trying to control specialised care costs and in estimating annual budgets more precisely although this has led to care budgets being made too tight.

Innovative Policies

Each local authority in Finland is expected to have an up-to-date policy strategy on care for older people that safe-guards their social rights. It has been recommended that the strategy contain a service development programme, which ensures a good quality of life for the older person, their self-determination and independence, regardless of their functional capacity.

Finland also offers support for informal caregivers. Relatives (a spouse, partner, children) who care and see after an older person are entitled to an allowance for this care. This is provided by the municipality. Municipalities may also arrange various social and health services to back up this care. These are arranged when the relevant local authority and the person providing the care come together and draw up a care agreement that includes a plan for care and services. In 2004, the minimum allowance received by caregivers was €229.29 a month. The caregiver who has made an agreement with the municipalities is entitled to an employment pension accrual, providing that he/she is not already on pension and they are also entitled to two free days a month during a period of time that the nature of the care they are providing is very demanding. During this statutory free time, the municipality is responsible to provide care to the older recipient.

France

Current Policy

In terms of care services, institutions for older people are divided into medical and welfare institutions. Welfare institutions include social establishments like shelter homes and nursing/ residential homes, which are basically collective housing, offering a range of non-medical facilities (such as catering and laundry) and infirmary services, while medical institutions mostly represent long-term care hospitals.

The French home-care policy has developed a large number of services, to assist in activities of daily living, to provide nursing and medical care at home, to improve living conditions, to maintain social relationships and to postpone institutional-isation and hospitalisation. The main homecare services are 'home-helpers' and the 'home-care service' performed by a number of nurses, assistant-nurses and physiotherapists. Access to home-care is determined by eligibility and level of dependence of the older person. Dependency being defined as: 'the need for a third party to assist in activities of daily living'.

Care of older people is financed by health insurance funds for institutional care and by the older people themselves, for residential care. The costs of residential care can be quite high (€40-45 per day) and are generally borne by the patient. However provisions are made to those unable to afford this, for example their accommodation costs may be covered by the local councils.

Innovative Policies

France has a consumer-directed homecare programme, which is funded by local taxes. This programme allows the older person to hire, train, supervise and fire, if they feel it necessary, the home-care worker. This government programme gives consumers (the older person in need of care) rather than the homecare agencies control over who provides the care services and how they should be delivered. It empowers the user in terms of the type of care they receive and how they should receive it. However, there has been criticism of this programme[21]. Tilly et al highlighted that stakeholders in this programme have almost universally condemned the French programme's

bureaucracy and inefficiency – the programme has a means-testing procedure that involves a complicated calculation of the rental value of assets as part of income. In this regard, processing the procedure is very slow.

France views the family as having an important role in the care of older people. According to a 1999 report[22], there has been renewed governmental interest in the role of the family in terms of care for older people. This is partly to do with the concern to curb social security spending, but it is also partly to do with the social characteristics of the French population, as many children in France feel a moral obligation to care for their older parents.

Netherlands

Current Policy

The Netherlands has the highest rate of residential care in Europe for older people in nursing homes and psychiatric hospitals. It has a comprehensive set of services for those who need long term care. But it has become less popular over the last 30 years and there has been a noticeable decline in the number of older people who come to stay in long term care.

The Netherlands has wide-ranging homecare services; these services include the provision of transport, wheelchairs and special facilities in the home of the older person.[23] Eligibility to these services is assessed by persons independent of those involved in the provision and funding of care; it is based on a set of standardised procedures. As a result of the comprehensive homecare services offered, more and more older people are now choosing to remain living in their own homes, as they grow older. As a consequence, the HiT (2004)[24] report found that the average age of new residents entering into residential or nursing homes is now above 80 years and increasing.

21. Tilly et al (2000) 'Consumer-Directed Home and Community Services Programs in Five Countries: Policy Issues for Older People and Government'.

22. Breuil-Genier (1999) 'Caring for the Dependent Older people: More informal than formal', INSEE Studies.

23. http://www.minibuza.nl/default.asp?CMS_ITEM=MBZ426386

24. 'Health Care Systems in Transition – Netherlands' (2004) WHO Regional Office for Europe on behalf of European Observatory on Health Systems and Policies

Long-term and homecare services are subsidised by the government via the Exceptional Medical Expenses Act and personal budgets for homecare. People can choose a residential home of their liking if they cover all the costs themselves. If people are not able to cover the costs themselves, then the person is referred to and applies for a place to the *Municipal Committees on Needs Assessment*. A social worker or nurse then starts the admission process (HiT, 2004).

Innovative Policies

The Dutch are committed to providing services which are of high quality and allow the older person to remain living independently. In response to this, residential and nursing homes in the Netherlands have recently started to provide, new types of integrated services, including meals-on-wheels; alarm systems for older people living in the community; temporary admissions to those who have been recently in hospital if their partner/spouse is unable to care for them immediately after their discharge from hospital; respite care for overloaded care givers; and day care.

Like France, the Netherlands also has a consumer-directed homecare programme. This enables the older person (the consumer) to choose and design their own homecare package, which they think would best suit their needs. The programme is intended to empower the consumer to choose and manage their own care. Family care givers play a vital role in the programme, as 60% of the care-givers involved in the programme were related in some way to the person in need of care. This is recognised and integrated into the formal care structure of the programme and is subsidised as part of the care package (i.e. families can be employed as 'carers').

Sweden

Current Policy

Sweden offers institutional long-stay care for older people in the form of nursing homes. There has been a focus recently on making these homes as much like home as possible; for example, in all homes now every patient has their own bedroom. Specialised accommodation, where older people live in 'supported accommodation' suitable to their needs, while being able to remain independent, have also been provided in Sweden. This type of accommodation is suitable to those with extensive needs but wish to remain living independently. Institutional care and specialised accommodation are arranged and provided by the Swedish municipalities.

Homecare services are also provided to those who wish to remain living in their own homes. The basic principle of Swedish homecare is that everyone who would like to remain living in their own homes in spite of illness or diminished capacity should be offered support and care in order to do so. To achieve this, Sweden now provides extensive homecare services. Special nursing staff make home visits and provide necessary services 24 hours a day. Home assistance services are also available around the clock and these include shopping, cleaning, cooking, washing and personal hygiene for those who cannot cope on their own. In the last five years, these services have changed to become more care-oriented and less aimed at providing general services[25].

Generally, the Swedish care system is considered to be of a high quality. The care services provided, as mentioned above, include nursing home/residential care as well as homecare services and are, according to the HiT report, adequate and of a good quality.

---

25. 'Health Care in Transition – Sweden' (2001), WHO Regional Office for Europe on behalf of European Observatory on Health Systems and Policies.

Innovative Policies

In Sweden, policy aims to enable older people to live independently with a high quality of life. The Swedish Riksday (government) has outlined a number of objectives for national policy in regard to older people, these objectives include:

— to be able to live an active life and have influence over their everyday lives;

— to be able to grow in security and retain their independence;

— to be treated with respect; and

— have access to good health care and social services.

One of the most important principals of Swedish policy is that any initiatives relating to older people are framed in such a way that the older person can continue living in their own homes for as long as possible, even when an intensive level of care is needed.[26]

While regional municipalities are financially responsible for the care they provide to older people, they do charge for the services older people receive. Consequently fees vary across regions, according to the number of hours of help the person receives. Fees cannot exceed real cost and they are not subsidised so the patient only pays part of the cost. There has been a trend towards de-centralisation in Sweden, so each municipality has the power to choose what kind of services they will provide to older people in their particular jurisdiction and whether they will provide these services themselves or may choose to purchase these services from the private market. As previously mentioned, purchasing care services has become increasingly popular in recent years. According to the HiT report (2001), about half the municipalities in Sweden now use private companies to provide care services to older people. The private market is most commonly used to provide nursing home and residential care. This has taken place in response to the fiscal crisis experienced in Sweden during the 1990s. Contracting out

services is seen as a way of curbing public spending, which has been on the agenda of the municipalities since the 1990s.

For those who care for older people on an informal basis, Sweden offers three types of support: respite and relief services, support and educational groups for carers and economic support for caring. Informal carers are also entitled to a number of cash benefits and the carer can be directly employed by the municipality to care for older people. This system is mostly used when the caregiver is of working age and in sparsely populated areas (OECD, 2005).

In Sweden, a parliamentary committee in regard to older people has also been set up called *Senior Citizen 2005*; its main aim is to lay the groundwork for the long-term development of policies for older people. The committee is made up of 17 members representing the political composition of the Swedish parliament and it is advised by experts from a number of relevant government authorities and organisations. This committee views ageing as a dynamic process with scope for variation and individual development and so is committed to producing concepts on ageing that are as varied and dynamic as the process itself. *Senior Citizen 2005* is also committed to promoting opportunities for people to develop at all stages of their lives.[27]

New Zealand

Current Policy

New Zealand provides long-term institutional care for older people in the form of residential/nursing home care and hospital care. Recently, there has been a move towards greater use of residential care for rehabilitation in the hope that some may recover sufficiently to be discharged and live independently again.

26. Ministry of Health and Social Affairs (2001) 'Policy for the older people', Sweden.

27. Senior Citizen (2005), 'Policies for the older people: a vision of the future', Sweden.

Homecare is offered to those who wish to remain living in their own home and are in need of care. Some of the services available include transport services and health and safety awareness programmes. Older people are assessed for homecare services through needs assessment.

Residential care is partly funded by the Department of Health on the basis of entitlement and partly funded by the older person in residential care. Each resident contributes their Superannuation entitlement and may contribute more, depending on their income and assets. Homecare services are funded by the Department of Health on the basis of entitlement. Expenditure on homecare services has more than doubled in the period of 2003-2004[28].

The New Zealand Government also recognises the importance of the role of the informal carer and acknowledges that the policy of encouraging older people to remain living in their own home, has led to a greater dependency on family and friends. In response to this, the Government has increased its expenditure on carer support and respite care services, over the last five years (*Report of the Working Party on Support Services for Older People*, 2005).

Innovative Policies

New Zealand has developed the *Positive Aging Strategy* which underlines the Government's commitment to promote the value and participation of older people in society. The main aim of this Strategy is to improve the opportunities for older people to participate in the community in ways they choose. The Strategy provides a framework within which all policy with implications for older people can be commonly understood and developed, and to ensure that future ageing policies will empower older people to make choices that will enable

them to live a satisfying and healthy life, provide opportunities for older people to participate in and contribute to family and community, and ensure that older people live in a safe and secure environment and receive the services they need to do so.

The Strategy also recognises that 'ageing in place' is closely linked to positive ageing; that older people should be able to make choices in later life about where to live, and receive the support needed to do so. The Strategy believes that for older people to maintain their independence and age in place successfully, it is important that they have adequate and affordable housing that meets their needs. It is in everybody's best interests, the Strategy states, that 'older people are supported and encouraged to remain self-reliant and to remain actively involved in the well-being of themselves and their families, friends and the wider community'.

The Strategy believes that the benefits of positive ageing for individuals are numerous; they include good health, self-fulfilment and intellectual stimulation. Positive ageing is good for society as a whole too.

The goals of this *Positive Aging* Strategy include:

— to make sure that all older people have secure and adequate income;

— to provide a holistic range of health services that are affordable, effective and accessible;

— to provide a set of housing options to older people that are both affordable and appropriate to their housing needs;

— to provide affordable and accessible transport options to older people;

— to ensure that older people feel safe and secure in their own homes;

— to make sure older people living in rural communities are not disadvantaged when accessing services;

28. *Report of the Working Party on Support Services for Older People & People with Disabilities (2005)* –
http://www.beehive.govt.nz/Document/Files/Working%20Party%20Report%20on%20Support%20Services.pdf

— to educate the public on the benefits of older people so that all will have positive attitudes;

— to eliminate ageism in the workplace and encourage employers to employ older people; and

— to increase the opportunities for personal growth and community participation for the older person.[29]

In 2004, the New Zealand Government launched a report[30] on progress that has been achieved since the Strategy was initiated in 2001. The report states that the Government has implemented a number of measures as recommended by the Strategy. These include:

— legislation to progressively remove asset testing from residential care was introduced into the New Zealand Parliament;

— guidelines for multidisciplinary, comprehensive and integrated assessment processes for older people and their carers was developed and published;

— funding was provided to three community groups specifically to build 20 new specialised housing units for older people; and

— the Government has provided $4 million (about €2.26 million) to a university in New Zealand to carry out research into well-being and ageing.

---

29. *Ministry of Senior Citizens (2001) 'The New Zealand Positive Ageing Strategy: Towards a Society for all Ages'.*

30. *Ministry of Senior Citizens (2004) 'The New Zealand Positive Ageing Strategy: Annual Report 2003-2004'.*

Annex 5   Care for Older People Plenary Session, Royal Hospital Kilmainham, Wednesday 28th September 2005

Attendance List

Name	Organisation
Ms Eilish Ashe	Inch Community Council
Cllr Ger Barron	General Council of County Councils
Ms Wendy Bass	Dunlaoghaire-Rathdown County Council
Mr Ilija Batljan	Advisor to the Swedish Government
Ms Roisin Boland	Irish Health Services Accreditation Board
Ms Carmel Brennan	Macra na Feirme
Ms Bernie Broderich	Duagh Family Resource Centre Ltd
Ms Regina Buckley	HSE
Ms Margaret Buckley	Gerontological Nursing
Ms Paula Carey	ICTU
Ms Eithne Carey	FARA
Deputy Pat Carey	Fianna Fáil
Mr Bob Carroll	National Council on Ageing & Older People
Mr Alan Carthy	Fingal County Council
Ms Maureen Chalmers	WISE
Ms Angela Coleman	Older Womens Network
Mr Jim Collier	FARA
Mr Noel Collins	
Mr Paul Costello	Irish Nursing Homes Association
Cllr Peter Coyle	
Ms Sheila Cronin	CORI
Mr Donal Crowley	Johnstown Killiney Active Retirement Association
Dr Nell Crushell	HSE - Southern Area
Deputy John Curran	Fianna Fáil
Ms Bernadine da Cunha	
Ms Tara Deacy	Ballyfermot Partnership
Mr Michael Doody	ICMSA
Ms Teresa Downey	Dublin City Council
Ms Martha Doyle	Trinity College
Ms Breda Dunlea	FARA
Ms Frances Dunne	Dublin City Council
Mr Joe Egner	HSE
Mr Henning Ennall	Swedish Ambassador to Ireland
Ms Niamh Fitzgerald	Department of Social and Family Affairs
Ms Maura Fitzgerald	Castlemaine Community Services
Ms Áine Flynn	Our Lady's Hospice
Ms Mo Flynn	HSE Eastern Region
Ms Maria Fox	Disability Federation of Ireland
Mr Frank Goodwin	The Carers Association
Ms Louise Halloran	

Ms Maeve Halpin	CARE Local
Cllr Constance Hanniffy	General Council of County Councils
Ms Mairead Hayes	Senior Citizens Parliament
Ms Evelyn Hayes	IFA
Ms Kathleen Herlihy	The Alzheimer Society
Mr Liam Herrick	Irish Human Rights Commission
Ms Joan Holden	Irish Country Womens Association
Mr Gerard Hughes	Economic and Social Research Institute
Mr Brian Judd	Federation of Acitve Retirement Associations
Ms Cáit Keane	
Ms Angela Keegan	The Alzheimer Society of Ireland
Mr Donal Kelly	HSE Eastern Region
Ms Anne Labrosse	Meitheal Mhuscrai
Mr John Laffan	Dept of the Environment, Heritage & Local Government
Ms Eileen Leen	Blennerville Active Retirement Association
Ms Kate Levey	Department of Finance
Mr Finbarr Long	Housing Dept, Cork City Council
Ms Heidi Lougheed	IBEC
Ms Betty Lynch	
Mr Paul Maher	Age & Opportunity
Ms Ursula Manning	
Mr Ian Martin	Martin Services Ltd
Mrs Josephine McCague	Whitehall Active Retirement Group
Cllr Patricia McCarthy	Association of Municipal Authorities of Ireland
Ms Mary McDermott	Health Service Executive
Ms Betty McElwaine	Older Women's Network (Ireland)
Ms Anne-Marie McGauran	Institute of Public Adminstration
Ms Catherine McGuigan	Fold TeleCare
Ms Grace McGuire	Dublin City Council
Ms Mary McKeon	Department of Finance
Ms Linda McKernan	Muintir na Tíre
Ms Mary McNutt	Cuanross
Mr Frank Mills	HSE South West Area
Mr Kevin Molloy	FARA
Senator Paschal Mooney	Fianna Fáil
Dr Ken Mulpeter	Letterkenny General Hospital
Ms Geraldine Murphy	Finglas Cabra Partnership
Dr Kathy Murphy	NUI Galway
Mr Eugene Murray	The Irish Hospice Foundation
Ms Aoife O'Brien	The Women's Health Council
Ms Eleanor O'Brien	Tallaght Equal Assists (Tallaght Partnership)
Ms Donna O'Brien	Community Services
Ms Brigid O'Brien	Health Service Executive
Ms Mary O'Donnell	NMPDU, HSE Eastern Region

Dr Fergus O'Ferrall	The Adelaide Hospital Society
Mr Michael O'Halloran	Irish Senior Citizens Parliament
Ms Orla O'Hanlon	The Atlantic Philanthropies (Ireland) Ltd
Ms Mary Lou O'Kennedy	Emergency Response Ltd
Prof. Des O'Neill	
Prof. Eamon O'Shea	NUI Galway
Mr Donal J. O'Sullivan	The Tralee '97 Probus Club
Ms Nora O'Sullivan	Dominican Day Centre
Mr Patrick O'Toole	National Council on Ageing & Older People
Ms Mary Power	Irish Nurses Organisation
Ms Sinead Quill	National Council on Ageing & Older People
Sr Brigid Reynolds	CORI
Ms Louise Richardson	Older Women's Network (Ireland)
Ms Dorothy Robinson	FARA
Ms Anne-Marie Ross	Department of Health & Children
Ms Hilary Scanlan	Health Service Executive
Mr Tom Sexton	National Federation Pensioners Association
Mr Michael Shiell	Abbey Health Care Ltd
Ms Sheila Simmons	Irish Association of Older People
Mr Dermot Smyth	Department of Health & Children
Mr David Stratton	Age Action Ireland Ltd
Dr John Sweeny	NESC
Dr Cillian Twomey	Irish Gerontrological Society
Ms Aisling Walsh	The Disability Federation of Ireland
Mr Seamus Walsh	FARA
Mr Kieran Walsh	M. & O.E Department
Senator Kate Walsh	Progressive Democrats
Mr Brendan Ward	NESDO
Mr Robin Webster	Age Action Ireland
Deputy Michael Woods	Fianna Fáil
Ms Margaret Wrenn	Duagh Family Resource Centre Ltd

Terms of Reference and Constitution of the NESF

1. The role of the NESF will be:

— to monitor and analyse the implementation of specific measures and programmes identified in the context of social partnership arrangements, especially those concerned with the achievement of equality and social inclusion; and

— to facilitate public consultation on policy matters referred to it by the Government from time to time.

2. In carrying out this role the NESF will:

— consider policy issues on its own initiative or at the request of the Government; the work programme to be agreed with the Department of the Taoiseach, taking into account the overall context of the NESDO;

— consider reports prepared by Teams involving the social partners, with appropriate expertise and representatives of relevant Departments and agencies and its own Secretariat;

— ensure that the Teams compiling such reports take account of the experience of implementing bodies and customers/clients including regional variations;

— publish reports with such comments as may be considered appropriate;

— convene meetings and other forms of relevant consultation appropriate to the nature of issues referred to it by the Government from time to time.

3. The term of office of members of the NESF will be three years. During the term alternates may be nominated. Casual vacancies will be filled by the nominating body or the Government as appropriate and members so appointed will hold office until the expiry of the current term of office of all members. Retiring members will be eligible for re-appointment.

4. The Chairperson and Deputy Chairperson of the NESF will be appointed by the Government.

5. Membership of the NESF will comprise 15 representatives from each of the following four strands:

— the Oireachtas;

— employer, trade unions and farm organisations;

— the voluntary and community sector; and

— central government, local government and independents.

6. The NESF will decide on its own internal structures and working arrangements.

Membership of the NESF

Independent Chairperson	Dr Maureen Gaffney
Deputy Chairperson	Mary Doyle, Dept. of the Taoiseach

Strand (i) Oireachtas

Fianna Fáil	Michael Woods T.D.
	Pat Carey T.D.
	John Curran T.D.
	Senator Mary O'Rourke
	Senator Paschal Mooney
	Senator Brendan Daly
	Senator Geraldine Feeney
Fine Gael	Senator Paul Coghlan
	Damien English T.D.
	Paul Kehoe T.D.
Labour	Joan Burton T.D.
	Willie Penrose T.D.
Progressive Democrats	Senator Kate Walsh
Independents	Senator Feargal Quinn
Technical Group	Jerry Cowley T.D.

Strand (ii) Employer/Trade Unions/Farming Organisations

Employer/Business Organisations

IBEC	Maria Cronin
	Heidi Lougheed
Small Firms' Association	Patricia Callan
Construction Industry Federation	Dr Peter Stafford
Chambers of Commerce/ Tourist Industry/Exporters Association	Seán Murphy

Trade Unions

Technical Engineering & Electrical Union	Eamon Devoy
Civil & Public Service Union	Blair Horan
AMICUS	Jerry Shanahan
SIPTU	Manus O'Riordan
ITCU	Paula Carey

Agricultural/Farming Organisations

Irish Farmers' Association	Mary McGreal
Irish Creamery Milk Suppliers' Association	Michael Doody
Irish Co-Operative Organisation Society	Mary Johnson
Macra na Feirme	Carmel Brennan
Irish Country Women's Association	Anne Murray

Strand (iii) Community and Voluntary Sector

Womens Organisations

National Women's Council of Ireland	Orla O'Connor
	Dr Joanna McMinn

Unemployed

INOU	John Farrell
ICTU Centres for the Unemployed	Patricia Short

Disadvantaged

CORI	Sr Brigid Reynolds
Society of St. Vincent de Paul	Audry Deane
Pavee Point	Bríd O'Brien
Anti-Poverty Networks	Joe Gallagher

Youth/Children

NYCI	Marie Clarie McAleer
Children's Rights Alliance	Jillian Van Turnhout

Older People

Senior Citizen's Parliament/Age Action	Robin Webster

Disability

Disability Federation of Ireland	Aisling Walsh

Others

The Carers' Association	Frank Goodwin
Irish Rural Link	Seamus Boland
The Wheel	Fergus O'Ferrall

Strand (iv) Central Government, Local Government and Independents

Central Government

Secretary-General, Department of Finance

Secretary-General, Department of Enterprise, Trade and Employment

Secretary-General, Department of Social and Family Affairs

Secretary-General, Department of Community, Rural and Gaeltacht Affairs

Secretary-General, Dept. of the Environment, Heritage and Local Government

Local Government

General Council of County Councils	Councillor Ger Barron
	Councillor Jack Crowe
	Councillor Constance Hanniffy
Association of Municipal Authorities	Councillor Patricia McCarthy
County and City Managers Association	John Tierney

Independents:

Geary Institute, UCD	Prof Colm Harmon
Department of Sociology, NUI Maynooth	Dr Mary P. Corcoran
ESRI	Prof Brian Nolan
Tansey, Webster, Stewart & Company Ltd.	Paul Tansey
	Cáit Keane

Secretariat

Director	Seán Ó hÉigeartaigh
Policy Analysts	David Silke
	Gerard Walker
Executive Secretary	Paula Hennelly

NESF Publications

(i) NESF Reports

Report No.	Title	Date
1.	Negotiations on a Successor Agreement to the PESP	Nov 1993
2.	National Development Plan 1994 – 1999	Nov 1993
3.	Commission on Social Welfare - Outstanding recommendations	Jan 1994
4.	Ending Long-term Unemployment	June 1994
5.	Income Maintenance Strategies	July 1994
6.	Quality Delivery of Social Services	Feb 1995
7.	Jobs Potential of Services Sector	April 1995
8.	First Periodic Report on the Work of the Forum	May 1995
9.	Jobs Potential of Work Sharing	Jan 1996
10.	Equality Proofing Issues	Feb 1996
11.	Early School Leavers and Youth Unemployment	Jan 1997
12.	Rural Renewal - Combating Social Exclusion	Mar 1997
13.	Unemployment Statistics	May 1997
14.	Self-Employment, Enterprise and Social Inclusion	Oct 1997
15.	Second Periodic Report on the Work of the Forum	Nov 1997
16.	A Framework for Partnership – Enriching Strategic Consensus through Participation	Dec 1997
17.	Enhancing the Effectiveness of the Local Employment Service	Mar 2000
18.	Social and Affordable Housing and Accommodation: Building the Future	Sept 2000
19.	Alleviating Labour Shortages	Nov 2000
20.	Lone Parents	July 2001
21.	Third Periodic Report on the Work of the Forum	Nov 2001
22.	Re-integration of Prisoners	Jan 2002
23.	A Strategic Policy Framework for Equality Issues	Mar 2002
24.	Early School Leavers	Mar 2002
25.	Equity of Access to Hospital Care	July 2002
26.	Labour Market Issues for Older Workers	Feb 2003
27.	Equality Policies for Lesbian, Gay and Bisexual People: Implementation Issues	April 2003
28.	The Policy Implications of Social Capital	June 2003
29.	Equality Policies for Older People	July 2003
30.	Fourth Periodic Report on the Work of the NESF	Nov 2004
31.	Early Childhood Care and Education	Sept 2005

(ii) NESF Opinions

Opinion No.	Title	Date
1.	Interim Report of the Task Force on Long-term Unemployment	Mar 1995
2.	National Anti-Poverty Strategy	Jan 1996
3.	Long-term Unemployment Initiatives	Apr 1996
4.	Post PCW Negotiations – A New Deal?	Aug 1996
5.	Employment Equality Bill	Dec 1996
6.	Pensions Policy Issues	Oct 1997
7.	Local Development Issues	Oct 1999
8.	The National Anti-Poverty Strategy	Aug 2000

NESF Opinions under the Monitoring Procedures of Partnership 2000

Opinion No.	Title	Date
1.	Development of the Equality Provisions	Nov 1997
2.	Targeted Employment and Training Measures	Nov 1997

(iii) NAPS Social Inclusion Forum: Conference Reports

1.	Inaugural Meeting	Jan 2003
2.	Second Meeting of the NAPS Social Inclusion Forum	Jan 2005